KU-649-071

Contents

Chapter Eleven: The bloody Thirties

Chapter Twelve: For the sake of Ireland

Chapter Thirteen: The curtain drops

HANGED AT CRUMLIN ROAD GAOL

THE STORY OF CAPITAL PUNISHMENT IN BELFAST

STEVEN MOORE

COLOURPOINT BOOKS

Dedicated to the memory of my mother,
Eileen Moore, who as a child living in Perth Street,
off the Crumlin Road, used to play in the grounds of
the courthouse and happily wave at the
inmates inside the gaol.

Published 2013 by Colourpoint Books
an imprint of Colourpoint Creative Ltd
Colourpoint House, Jubilee Business Park
21 Jubilee Road, Newtownards, BT23 4YH
Tel: 028 9182 6339
Fax: 028 9182 1900
E-mail: info@colourpoint.co.uk
Web: www.colourpoint.co.uk

First Edition
Third Impression, 2018

A catalogue record for this book is available from the British Library.

Designed by April Sky Design, Newtownards
Tel: 028 9182 7195
Web: www.aprilsky.co.uk

Printed by GPS Colour Graphics Ltd, Belfast

ISBN 978-1-78073-049-3

Front cover: The front façade and entrance to the Crumlin Road Gaol.
Rear cover: A prison warden posed on the third level of the circle in the restored Gaol.
Frontispiece: The entrance archway in the gate lodge.

About the author: Steven Moore, formerly News Editor with the News Letter, the oldest English language daily newspaper in the world, and currently Deputy Editor of Farm Week, the leading agriculture newspaper in Northern Ireland, was born and educated in north Belfast, but has lived in Bangor, County Down, since 1982.

Acknowledgments

MANY PEOPLE HAVE HELPED in the preparation of this book. Friends, colleagues and in some cases complete strangers have gone out of their way to offer assistance in the search for information or photographs. To each I offer my sincere thanks.

The staff at the Central Library in Belfast, and in particular its Newspaper Library, have been exceedingly patient and helpful. Likewise, the librarians at the Linen Hall Library and the Bangor Branch Library, the latter doing all they could to supply what must have seemed like an endless list of requested books. I also spent many fascinating hours at the Public Record Office of Northern Ireland and thank the staff there.

Thanks must go to former Belfast High Sheriff Jim Walker and Robin Boyd at the City Hall for permission and assistance respectively to go through the council files, and to the Presbyterian Church for access to its collection of the *Witness* newspaper.

There are several individuals connected with the Prison Service who it would be imprudent to name but without whose help the task would have been immeasurably more difficult and less rewarding.

I owe a special debt of gratitude to Mike McComb, former head librarian at the *News Letter*, who allowed me free access to the bound volumes in his care and kindly gave permission for a number of photographs to be reproduced, and to Kathleen Bell, former librarian at the *Irish News*, who likewise cheerfully produced requested photos and granted permission for their use.

Many of the illustrations have been supplied by the Ulster Museum, the National Library of Ireland and the Public Record Office of Northern Ireland. In addition, can I thank Fr Frank Donnelly, formerly parish priest of St Peter's Church, Drogheda, for the photograph taken by himself of the head of Oliver Plunkett, and the National Graves Association for the picture of hanged IRA man Tom Williams.

My brother-in-law William Stockdale, who gave freely of his time and considerable photographic skills to supply many of the illustrations, deserves particular credit.

Last, but not least, I must thank my wife Heather who, in addition to proof reading, listened without complaint to me talking endlessly about this or that aspect of hanging.

It is inevitable that inaccuracies slip into a work of this nature. For those, I alone take responsibility.

Steven Moore

Publisher's Note

The publisher gratefully acknowledges the assistance of:

Kieran Quinn and the staff of the Crumlin Road Gaol Visitor Attraction and Conference Centre

Deputy Keeper of the Records, Public Record Office of Northern Ireland

Record of Executions

William Magill	Cornmarket	9 June 1798	United Irishman
James Dickey	Cornmarket	28 June 1798	United Irishman
John Storey	Cornmarket	30 June 1798	United Irishman
Hugh Grimes	Cornmarket	5 July 1798	United Irishman
Henry Byers	Cornmarket	11 July 1798	United Irishman
Henry Joy McCracken	Cornmarket	17 July 1798	United Irishman
John Doe	Castle Place	6 September 1816	Weaver
John Magill	Castle Place	6 September 1816	Weaver
Robert O'Neill	Crumlin Road Gaol	21 June 1854	Soldier
Daniel Ward	Crumlin Road Gaol	8 April 1863	Carpenter
John Daly	Crumlin Road Gaol	26 April 1876	Coal porter
Arthur McKeown	Crumlin Road Gaol	14 January 1889	Car driver
John Gilmour	Crumlin Road Gaol	17 August 1894	Farmer
William Woods	Crumlin Road Gaol	11 January 1901	Dealer
Richard Justin	Crumlin Road Gaol	19 August 1909	Labourer
Simon McGeown	Crumlin Road Gaol	17 August 1922	Labourer
Michael Pratley	Crumlin Road Gaol	8 May 1924	Tailor
William Smiley	Crumlin Road Gaol	8 August 1928	Farm labourer
Samuel Cushnan	Crumlin Road Gaol	8 April 1930	Farm labourer
Thomas Dornan	Crumlin Road Gaol	31 July 1931	Farmer
Eddie Cullens	Crumlin Road Gaol	13 January 1932	Showman
Harold Courtney	Crumlin Road Gaol	7 April 1933	Lorry driver
Thomas Williams	Crumlin Road Gaol	2 September 1942	Labourer
Samuel McLaughlin	Crumlin Road Gaol	25 July 1961	Foundry worker
Robert McGladdery	Crumlin Road Gaol	20 December 1961	Labourer

We waited for the stroke of eight:
  Each tongue was thick with thirst:
For the stroke of eight is the stroke of Fate
  That makes a man accursed,
And Fate will use a running noose
  For the best man and the worst.

We had no other thing to do,
  Save to wait for the sign to come:
So, like things of stone in a valley lone,
  Quiet we sat and dumb:
But each man's heart beat thick and quick
  Like a madman on a drum!

With sudden shock the prison-clock
  Smote on the shivering air,
And from all the gaol rose up a wail
  Of impotent despair,
Like the sound that frightened marshes hear
  From a leper in his lair.

And as one sees most fearful things
  In the crystal of a dream,
We saw the greasy hempen rope
  Hooked to the blackened beam,
And heard the prayer the hangman's snare
  Strangled into a scream.

And all the woe that moved him so
  That he gave that bitter cry,
And the wild regrets, and the bloody sweats,
  None knew so well as I:
For he who lives more lives than one
  More deaths than one must die.

**Extract from *The Ballad of Reading Gaol*
by Oscar Wilde**

INTRODUCTION

Behind the garden wall

Which is more immoral; which is more inhuman? For the State legally and deliberately to execute a convicted murderer or to see further innocent lives being taken because the murderer is spared the supreme penalty?

Lord Dunleath during the capital punishment debate in December 1974

Behind the garden wall, deep within the grounds of Her Majesty's Prison Belfast, popularly known as Crumlin Road Gaol, lie the remains of fifteen of the seventeen men who paid the ultimate price for their crimes on the gallows. It has been more than fifty years since the last body, placed in a plain softwood coffin, was lowered into its unmarked grave. There is no longer any garden behind the wall, the vegetable plots having given way to a tarmac car park for prison staff and later still providing additional parking for visitors to the neighbouring Mater Hospital.

Capital punishment came comparatively late to Belfast. Indeed, it took a revolution, in 1798, to precipitate the first executions. However, when it became the county town of Antrim, succeeding Carrickfergus, it took on the mantle as the official place of state justice and punishment, with a state-of-the-art county courthouse and gaol built on opposite sides of the Crumlin Road. The change followed a rapid growth in Belfast's population, which was approaching 90,000 in 1850 and had grown to 350,000 half a century later. Housing, sanitation and other facilities and amenities failed to keep pace and much of the town consisted of hovels where morality and respect for law and order were of scant regard. Crime escalated rapidly and for most of the nineteenth century the county assizes were dominated by business from

The County Gaol for Antrim, Crumlin Road, Belfast, about 1870. Completed in 1845, there were to be seventeen executions within its walls in the next 120 years. (© *National Museums Northern Ireland, Collection Ulster Museum, BELUM.Y7226*)

Belfast, leading to the creation of a 'County of the City of Belfast Assizes' specifically to deal with it.

The first execution at the Crumlin Road Gaol was in 1854, the last in 1961. Initially those hanged had committed their crimes in County Antrim, but following partition, in 1921, the gaol became the final destination of all those guilty of capital crimes in Northern Ireland who were to face the gallows. All those executed within the precincts of Belfast gaol were convicted murderers and all were from working class backgrounds. There were labourers and farmers, a soldier, an IRA man, an American Jew, an alcoholic tramp, a lorry driver and a car driver, this last of the horse-drawn variety. Several of the killings revolved around the pregnancy of unmarried girls, and the shame that involved in less enlightened times. Sex, in a much more ugly form, was the motive in other murders, while robbery, jealousy and resentment borne of bullying accounted for the rest. In many instances the guilt of the hanged man appears unquestionable and was often supported by an admission on the eve of execution. In other cases it is not so clear-cut.

Over its century and a half of existence, an estimated 25,000 prisoners made their way through the tunnel under the Crumlin Road from the gaol to the courthouse. The prison has played host to all sorts over those years, men, women and children, from murderers to bad-debtors, child criminals to political activists, lunatics to would-be suicide victims. Inmates included

HM Prison Belfast as it was in the 1990s, shortly before its closure as a working gaol. The four wings radiate from the circle area, allowing for easy observation. *(Prison Service)*

The ground floor of C Wing as it was in the 1990s. It was at the end of this wing that the scaffold was permanently housed from the start of the twentieth century. *(Prison Service)*

One-time Ulster Volunteer Force leader Gusty Spence served his sentence for murder in Crumlin Road Gaol. *(Irish News)*

Suffragette prisoners, who were housed in the gaol's A wing prior to the First World War; Éamon de Valera, later to become premier of the Republic of Ireland, who was held in solitary confinement for a month after being arrested for entering Northern Ireland illegally; Ulster Volunteer Force leader Gusty Spence and leading republicans Martin Meehan and Gerry Kelly, the later going on to become a member of the Northern Ireland Assembly; Ian Paisley, former Democratic Unionist Party leader and the original First Minister of the Assembly; and Sinn Féin leader Gerry Adams, who resigned his Assembly seat to be elected to parliament in the Republic.

There have been a number of successful escapes from the prison. On 9 May 1927, three republicans serving time for murder, along with a fourth man, overpowered a warder, took his keys and revolver, and using knotted sheets scaled the prison walls to make good their escape; five republican internees calmly threw a rope with a hook attached over the wall of the exercise yard and scaled it to freedom on 7 June 1941; four prisoners escaped on 15 January 1943; and another IRA prisoner used knotted bed sheets to make it over the wall on Boxing Day, 1960. The biggest escape came in 1971 when in November nine republican prisoners, armed with weapons smuggled into the gaol, escaped out on to the Crumlin Road, with a further three making it out of the gaol less than a month later. The last escape from the prison was on 10 June 1981, when one man got away.

But for all its history it is the seventeen men who faced the executioner that figure large in the public imagination, and it is the visit to the condemned cell and the death chamber that still provides the highlight for most on their tour of what is now a hugely popular visitor attraction.

SECTION ONE

A Place in History

CHAPTER ONE

A brutal past

Boys, you need not be in such a hurry;
there can be no fun till I come.

Victim of the Carrick gallows

THE TAKING OF A life in retribution for an injustice pre-dated by centuries the arrival of the Normans in Ireland, an event that imported a system of laws from outside the island. Long before the birth of Christ the ancient Britons were throwing their enemies into pits or on to sinking sand to die and, though the Anglo-Saxons practiced hanging, other, often more crude, methods were common. The Normans, however, virtually put a stop to the execution of prisoners with the exception of those found guilty of conspiring against the Crown. Nine hundred years later, in 1965, the House of Commons did exactly the same. In between, countless thousands of people suffered the humiliation and excruciating pain of the hangman's rope, the vast majority of them victims of laws that condemned even petty criminals to the gallows.

The reintroduction of capital punishment in a general form followed the succession to the English throne of King John in 1199. A Royal Charter, issued in the wake of the monarch's visit to Ireland in 1210, extended the Common Law to the parts of the island under English control. Elsewhere in Ireland, of course, Gaelic law survived, particularly in Ulster, up until the early 1600s. Under native law, the killing of another person was considered a civil rather than a criminal offence, which could often be made good by the paying of compensation. Those found guilty of killing highly respected members of the community, or who were too poor to pay the tariff demanded, were often burnt alive, illustrating the part social standing could play in deciding who lived and who died. Likewise, public outrage could force an issue, such as in the case of a man hanged in 1197 for stealing from a church in Derry.

Over time Irish custom resulted in a watering down of the Common Law imported from England, with the death penalty for murder often downgraded to a fine. By the end of the thirteenth century this had become normal practice and very few people, least of all those of English descent, actually ended up on the gallows. The last province to experience English Common Law was Ulster, which remained the most Gaelic part of Ireland until the bloody Elizabethan conquest. By 1603 the Irish champion Hugh O'Neill had been defeated and in the same year Sir Arthur Chichester, who had ruthlessly and effectively applied Mountjoy's scorched earth policy, was rewarded with the grant of a patent for the lands around Belfast Castle where, in June 1597, the military garrison had been attacked by the Clandeboye O'Neills and, "all the English men in the ward were hanged and their throats cut, and their bowells cutt oute of their bellyes".

The most famous seventeenth century Irish victim of the gallows, however, was not hanged in his homeland but at that most notorious site of gruesome ritual, Tyburn. It was in December 1679 that Oliver Plunkett, Archbishop

Sir Arthur Chichester, who played a prominent role in the Elizabethan conquest of Ulster, was granted a patent to develop the lands around Belfast Castle. *(Historical Notices of Old Belfast and its Vicinity, Robert M Young, Belfast, 1896)*

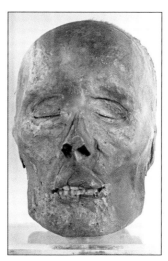

The head of Oliver Plunkett, cut from the body during the ritual dismemberment that followed his execution at Tyburn, was smuggled to Rome. It was eventually returned to Ireland and is now permanently housed in St Peter's Church, Drogheda. *(Fr Frank Donnelly)*

of Armagh, was arrested and imprisoned in Dublin Castle on a charge of high treason. Taken to London to stand trial, he was found guilty on the false evidence of two Franciscan monks. Sentenced to be hanged, drawn and quartered, he was taken to Tyburn on 1 July 1681, where the infamous executioner Jack Ketch half strangled him by allowing the cleric to swing from the noose for several minutes. He was then taken down, his heart and entrails wrenched from his body and burnt on the scaffold fire. The corpse was finally beheaded and cut into four pieces. The archbishop's remains, however, were not to rest in peace. The severed head was secretly removed from the scaffold during the bloody ritual of dismemberment and later turned up in Rome. In 1722 it was returned to Ireland and eventually placed in St Peter's Church, Drogheda, County Louth. The rest of the body was buried in the cemetery of St Giles in the Fields church in central London, but not before the arms had been amputated below the elbows as religious relics. The coffin was later exhumed and moved to a Benedictine abbey in Germany before being returned to England and St Gregory's Monastery, Bath, towards the end of the nineteenth century.

Oliver Cromwell, whose Roundhead army took Belfast in an assault on the North Gate in 1649, ended up on the scaffold after his death as Charles II desperately tried to avenge his father's execution. Illustration by John Carey. (*Historical Notices of Old Belfast and its Vicinity, Robert M Young, Belfast, 1896*)

Almost twenty years earlier at Tyburn, Oliver Cromwell, another name well remembered from Irish history, joined the list of those hanged on its gallows – despite already being dead. In 1662 the Roundhead who had terrorised much of Ireland was taken from his tomb in Westminster Abbey on the orders of Charles II, who desperately wanted revenge for his father's execution. Cromwell's body, plus the bodies of his son-in-law Henry Ireton and John Bradshaw, who had taken part in the trial and sentencing of Charles I, were hung from the Tyburn gallows for most of a day before being cut down, their heads removed, placed on pikes, and displayed at Westminster Hall.

Such was the popularity of the rope as a means of meting out justice that an average of 2,000 people a year were being hanged in England alone during the reign of Henry VIII, with only marginally fewer under Elizabeth I. Likewise in Ireland, the gallows on Dublin's St Stephen's Green were seldom idle, providing regular entertainment for vast crowds of the lower classes who flocked to watch the spectacle. Belfast at that time was still in the shadow of Carrickfergus, a little further along the lough shore. Holding the principle position in County Antrim, Carrick was well equipped to provide the required facilities when it came to exercising the full rigours of the law. For many years its scaffold, situated on Gallows Green, was known as the Three Sisters as it consisted of three stone columns, three feet in diameter and 18 feet high. Wooden beams ran between them, allowing three criminals to be hanged at a time. In Robert Young's volume, *Ulster in '98*, John Coates, a one-time secretary to the Antrim Grand Jury, recalled vividly both the procedure and some of its victims:

> "The modus operandi was as follows: On leaving the gaol, the cart, of the old two-solid-wheel kind, with the coffin crossways on it, went first, with the hangman; then the condemned walked behind, and on each side a file of soldiers, fully armed. When the cart was drawn under the fatal beam, the prisoner stood on it with the clergyman, who prayed with him till the hangman put the noose over his head, pulled the cap down on his face, and gave the signal to withdraw the cart. At one execution a man was suspended so low that his foot touched the ground. A soldier stepped forward and caught up the limb, so as to let him choke comfortably. He was ever after called the 'Hangman'. On one occasion the boys were rushing along the hedges so as to get near the scaffold for a good view, when the criminal shouted to them, 'Boys, you need not be in such a hurry; there can be no fun till I come.'"

The Three Sisters was later dismantled and executions transferred to the

The Three Sisters scaffold, at Gallows Green on the outskirts of Carrickfergus, could despatch up to three victims at a time. *(Historical Notices of Old Belfast and its Vicinity, Robert M Young, Belfast, 1896)*

County Gaol in the town centre. By the beginning of the eighteenth century there were some fifty offences punishable by death in addition to murder, treason, arson and rape. The industrial revolution in England, with its emphasis on material wealth and property, led to a huge increase in lawlessness and a corresponding rise in harsh laws. As towns and cities mushroomed, so did the number of residents living in extreme poverty, many spending what little money they had on alcohol. To make ends meet, women often turned to prostitution or sent their children to work in the likes of the mills where child labour was routinely engaged. Pickpockets roamed the streets, thieves struck at will and the rural laneways were the stomping grounds of highwaymen and many other unsavoury characters. Parliament, pressed to take action, passed statutes by the dozen that were intended to stem the tide of criminality.

Over the next 100 years there came into being what was known as the Bloody Code, with more than 220 pieces of legislation containing provisions for capital sentences. Most were introduced to tackle a specific annoyance but were open to interpretation by the courts and as a consequence were applied to a multitude of offences. For example, the notorious Waltham Black Act, enacted by Parliament in response to a spate of poaching in Hampshire, was eventually invoked to create more than 350 capital offences, ranging from carrying an arm to having a blackened face, taking a fish, cutting down a cherry tree, stealing turnips or writing threatening letters. Likewise, the Larceny Law, passed to clamp down on burglary, was interpreted to cover the theft of anything over 12 pence in value.

The fault lay largely with the Common Law system itself, which left it to the judges to determine the scope of vaguely worded Acts. If one judge accepted that a certain offence fell within the bounds of a particular Act, others followed suit, and so the list of capital crimes grew. A particularly unpleasant aspect of judgments at this time was the stipulation of mutilations and other cruelties as part of the sentence. The most popular of these, particularly for those accused of treason, was to have the victim hanged, drawn and quartered. This involved stringing them up by the neck, for up to 10 minutes, so they suffered the pain of the rope without succumbing to strangulation. After being cut down, and while still alive, the executioner set about them with a knife, severing the genitals, cutting out the intestines and heart and burning them in front of the baying crowd. Finally the head was severed and the body cut into four quarters for display at a public place.

Fortunately, such ritual barbarity on the scaffold was gradually phased out, though even as late as 1789 the *News Letter* was still reporting:

> "The following persons were tried and found guilty at the assizes of Clonmel: Edmond Duggan, otherwise Crosskeen, for poisoning Catherine Gueray, to be hanged, quartered, and beheaded on Saturday the 28th instant. Alice Daniel, otherwise, Duggan his wife, for the life offence, to be strangled and burned to ashes the same day, James Keane, for a burglary, committed at Golden-bridge, to be hanged the same day. Philip Murray, for horse stealing, to be hanged on the 4th of April next."

Women were generally not hanged, drawn and quartered for fear it would offend the spectators, being usually burnt at the stake instead. The Alice Daniel mentioned above was one of the last to suffer this form of execution, however, as it was repealed by Parliament the following year. A Bill passed in 1814 stipulated that drawing and quartering should be carried out only after the prisoner's death by hanging.

Newspaper reports at the end of the eighteenth century show just how common the death sentence was. At the Down Assizes in March 1789, for example, Patrick Campbell was found guilty of picking the pocket of James Smyth in Newry of £1 14s 8d and sentenced to be hanged on 9 May; at Omagh in April Thomas Hughes was found guilty of a double murder near Ballygawley which had already seen members of two families, the O'Donnellys and McGoughs, executed the previous year. Several months later Miles Donnelly was condemned to be hanged and beheaded for the same killing; also in April; and at the same court John McAfee was sentenced to be hanged for house-breaking, Pat Nugent for rape, and David Hog for robbery;

Belfast, *August* 18.

On Saturday laft, Edward Armftrong was execued at Downpatrick, purfuant to his fentence, for the un-natural murder of his own Infant. This unhappy cafe was rendered ftill more deplorable by the circum-ftance of his Wife having died very fuddenly and un-expectedly not long before. He declared that pover-ty was the caufe.

James Watfon Hull, Efq; High Sheriff of the county of Down, has been pleafed to appoint Mr. Robert Garrett of Lifburn to be his Under Sheriff, in the place of Mr. Robert Stewart, who, from bad health, has refigned; and Mr. Garrett was in confe-quence on Wednefday the 12th inft. fworn into office, before the Hon. Baron Hamilton at Downpatrick.

Belfast, *August* 21.

At the late Affizes for the county of Antrim, held at Carrickfergus, which ended on Monday laft, Jo-feph Blackwood of Belfaft, butcher, charged with the murder of George Emerfon on his return from Hillfborough Races—was acquitted. In confequence of an Appeal, by the next of kin, a new trial will be held in the Court of King's Bench, Dublin, on next Michaelmas term, which commences on the 3d day of November next.

At the fame Affizes, Hugh Giffen was found guilty on one indictment of ftealing three fheep; and on a fecond, for ftealing a firkin of butter, &c.—to be tranf-ported.

Edward Robinfon and John Knox were indicted for being loofe idle vagrants and vagabonds—to be tranfported purfuant to the ftatutes, unlefs they give fecurity within fix months to be of the peace and keep good behaviour.

James Orr the elder and James Orr the younger, found guilty of ftealing from Mrs. Margaret Henry, at Ballymoney, one quarter of a hundred of potatoes, value fixpence, to be privately whipped, imprifoned one week, and to remain in jail until they fhall give fecurity before two magiftrates to be of the peace for three years.

Ulster courts regularly passed the sentence of death in the eighteenth century, though not all those who found themselves in the dock on capital charges ended up on the gallows. From the *News Letter*, 1789. *(Belfast Central Library, Newspaper Library)*

in May, Dan Doughterty was condemned to die at Londonderry Assizes for breaking into a house near Claudy with his face blackened, while Charles Stewart, caught with his hand in the pocket of some unfortunate on the stairs of the courthouse on the Saturday of the same assizes, was also sentenced to be hanged; in August, Edward Armstrong was found guilty of murdering

Members of the Royal Irish Constabulary, with presumably one of the sergeant's daughters, pose for the camera around 1890. The RIC took over from the Belfast force after the latter was accused of being sectarian in its handling of the 1864 riots. *(PRONI, T2630/1A)*

his infant son and executed a few days later. His wife had died suddenly shortly before and in court Armstrong had blamed his impoverished state for the killing. A woman sentenced to death for robbery in October 1789 was reprieved after claiming she was pregnant. A jury, consisting of 13 women stopped at random in the street, was formed to determine whether or not she was telling the truth. Fortunately for her, they found in favour of the "wretched looking creature, without shoe or stocking".

The tide was turning, however, with the 50 years preceding 1860 seeing the vast majority of statutes covering capital punishment being repealed. The following year, 1861, the Criminal Law Consolidation Act was passed. It reduced the number of capital crimes to just four: murder, treason, arson in docklands and piracy. The reasons for this about-turn were two-fold: a campaign by a dedicated group of Members of Parliament to reform the system and, perhaps more importantly since it created the security to allow change, the foundation by Sir Robert Peel of the modern police force in England in 1829. As far as policing was concerned, Ireland was leading the way. As Chief Secretary of Ireland, Peel had created the Peace Preservation

Force in 1814, though Dublin and a few other baronies had already their own forces as early as 1778. The 1836 reorganisation of the Irish Constabulary, formed some 14 years earlier, saw the absorption of the PPF and a variety of other units into the national police force, though Dublin, Belfast and Londonderry continued to have their own constabularies. In 1800, the Irish Parliament, as one of its last actions before being abolished, had passed the Belfast Police Act. The new force was to have a short and chequered history. It was heavily involved in putting down the riots in the town in 1832, 1857 and 1864. Following the last of these, a commission of inquiry produced a damning report of the way in which the police handled the disturbances and condemning the fact that the Belfast force had only a handful of Roman Catholics in its 160-strong ranks. In June 1865, its duties were taken over by the Royal Irish Constabulary.

In due course there were further refinements of the legal system. Public executions were abolished in 1868; the hanging of under-16s officially ended in 1908, though no one under 18 years of age had been executed in the previous 20 years; and mothers who killed their babies and pregnant women were excluded from the death penalty in 1922 and 1931 respectively. The last executions to take place in Britain were in 1964 when two men were hanged at the same time on the same day but in different prisons.

CHAPTER TWO

The first to die

*I am just going to do my last duty to my country. It can be
done as well on the scaffold as on the field.*

**Rebel leader Robert Emmet
(Executed September 1803)**

T HE SAVAGERY THAT FOLLOWED the rebellion of 1798 rivaled the
bloodletting and terror of the actual battles. The fighting had been marked
by confusion, disorganisation and disappointment for the rebels, whose
initial gains were quickly lost to the King's forces. Many of the insurgents
took to the hills or open countryside in a bid to escape capture, while others
returned to their homes in the hope that their parts in the uprising would be
overlooked or not realised. Although the main confrontations in Ulster had
been confined to comparatively small areas of counties Antrim and Down,
the retribution which followed spread far and wide.

Belfast, which had been under martial law prior to the hostilities for fear
it would be a key player in the rebellion everyone knew was threatening,
remained calm. The town's rebels, realising the strength of the garrison
stationed there, had largely left days previously to join their comrades in the
countryside. Nonetheless, the 1798 rebellion was to produce the first State
executions in the town, with at least six men hanged there that year.

Shortly after 2.00 am on 7 June 1798, the first shots of the uprising were fired
in a brief and inconclusive confrontation between troops and rebels in Larne,
County Antrim. Within days reports were circulating of uprisings across the
county. Rebels had attacked and taken Randalstown and Ballymena, and had

The Battle of Antrim, at which Henry Joy McCracken led his rebel forces in an unsuccessful bid to take the town. The illustration, by JW Carey, was drawn almost 100 years after the event. *(Historical Notices of Old Belfast and its Vicinity, Robert M Young, Belfast, 1896)*

only narrowly failed in their attempt to overpower the garrison at Antrim. On 9 June, the County Down insurgents struck at Saintfield. Undoubtedly feelings were running high in Belfast as news spread, accompanied, it may be assumed, by outlandish rumour. It was in such a climate that William Magill was to meet his fate on Saturday 9 June. Little is known about the man who was to be the first person executed in the town other than he was tried before a court martial on a charge of "swearing soldiers from their allegiance". His failure to recruit them to the United Irishmen's cause cost him his life. So eager were the soldiers to have him dispatched, and so teach the citizens of the town a lesson, that they didn't wait for a scaffold to be erected. Instead, a rope was attached to a lamppost outside the Market House, on the corner of Cornmarket and High Street, and Magill sent to meet his Maker from the end of it.

As the rebellion crumbled, the troops set about the task of rounding up the ringleaders. A prison ship was moored offshore in Belfast Lough while the town's army barracks, in Barrack Street, and the Donegall Arms Hotel, in what is today Castle Place, were used to house prisoners brought in from the outlying areas.

A young attorney named James Dickey, from Crumlin, was next to feel the noose about his neck. Found "sulking in a bog" close to Divis Mountain, on the fringes of Belfast, by a party of soldiers, he was brought into the town on 25 June 1798, to stand trial. The following day he was hauled in front of a court martial sitting in the Exchange Rooms (which today stand vacant at the corner of Waring Street and Donegall Street, opposite the Northern Whig building) and accused of rebellion and treason, to which he pleaded not guilty. Apparently unconcerned at the situation he found himself in, Dickey assured the court he would give them no trouble but would happily acknowledge the truth of any evidence given and contradict what he considered lies. In fact, he appears to have put little effort into defending himself, even failing to produce witnesses on his behalf despite the court agreeing to a delay to allow him to do so. During the trial it was alleged that Dickey had been seen on horseback, sword in hand, urging on the rebels. He was said to have used the sword to behead a William Crawford, despite the latter begging for mercy, and accused of advocating the putting to death of prisoners captured

The trials of the United Irishmen were held in the Exchange Rooms, built in 1769 for the fifth Earl of Donegall on the corner of North Street and Donegall Street, Belfast. A second floor was later added and for many years the building served as a bank. *(Author)*

at the Battle of Randalstown. The court martial was held over three days, and was adjourned several times. On the last day proceedings were suspended for several hours after Dickey turned up insensible, either through alcohol or, as was suspected, after having taken poison. Sufficiently revived, he was found guilty and sentenced to be hanged and his head cut off and placed on top of the Market House. General Nugent, military commander of the Northern District, declined to reverse the court's decision. At about 8.00 pm that evening, Thursday 28 June 1798, Dickey – dressed in a light-coloured coat and grey pantaloons – was brought to the place of execution, in front of the Market House, where he spent almost an hour talking and praying with the Rev Sinclair Kelburn. His whole attitude to his predicament, the *News Letter* reported, was "seeming indifference". It went on:

> "About nine o'clock, he mounted a temporary scaffolding, erected at the Market-house, when he asked for a drink of water, which having got, he requested his body would be given to his friends; the executioner then attempted to cover his face with a handkerchief, which prisoner would not allow and in a few moments after he was launched into eternity. After hanging some time, he was taken down and his head severed from his body, which the executioner holding up in his hand exclaimed "This is the head of a traitor". It was then affixed to a spike, and placed on the Market-house."

Dickey's head was not to remain alone atop the Market House for long. The following day the trial of John Storey, who had worked as a printer on the United Irishman's newspaper, *The Northern Star*, got under way. Storey, from Islandbawn, Muckamore, had been captured in a quarry close to his home. Several witnesses testified to having seen Storey taking an active part in the Battle of Antrim (which he undoubtedly had). Although the court was adjourned until the next morning, so that Storey's father could give evidence in his son's defence, he was subsequently found guilty of rebellion and treason. Again General Nugent declined to exercise his powers of mercy. Shortly after 2.00 pm on Saturday 30 June, Storey was brought to the Market House, where the Rev Baistow ministered to him. About 3.30 pm he climbed the steps of the scaffold to meet his fate. After hanging for 15 minutes, the body was taken down, the head cut off and a spike thrust into it so it could be placed in an adjacent corner to Dickey's.

A few days later, on 5 July, it was the turn of Hugh Grimes to face the court martial. He was accused of being a rebel leader at Creevy Rocks, where the County Down insurgents had amassed, and at the Battle of Ballynahinch.

Henry Joy McCracken who, despite being the Northern leader of the uprising, was spared the beheading of his corpse normally dealt out to traitors. *(© National Museums Northern Ireland, Collection Ulster Museum, III/McCracken, HJ)*

Brought to the scaffold at 3.00 pm, he spent an hour in devotion with the Rev Dobbs before being executed. After hanging for three-quarters of an hour, he was cut down and the body handed over to his friends for burial. On the same day that Grimes was tried, another man, Lambert Brice, was condemned to die at Dundonald for being a leader at Ballynahinch and for housebreaking.

The Rev Dobbs also comforted the next man to face the Belfast scaffold. Henry Byers, described as a very young man, was convicted of taking cattle from Mr Price's farm at Saintfield and driving them to the rebel camp at Ballynahinch. He was obviously familiar with the Price household, having recently married the daughter of a servant there. Possibly because of his youth, the court left it to Mr Price to decide whether he should be hanged or not. Price is reputed to have clapped the young man on the back, pointed to the gallows and the heads on spikes beyond, and told him (according to the Rev Thomas Ledlie Birch of Saintfield) to "go boldly for he should soon have plenty of his neighbours for company". Byers, after spending some time with the Rev Dodds, was duly executed on Monday 11 July 1798, and his head placed with the others on top of the Market House.

The most significant figure from the rebellion to mount the steps of the Belfast gallows was Henry Joy McCracken. The Northern leader of the uprising, McCracken could have been in no doubt as he dressed in his green uniform to take on the Crown forces just what failure would mean. Imprisoned in Dublin's Kilmainham Gaol for most of the previous year, he had seen other men pay the extreme penalty of the law for their political beliefs. He wrote to his sister, Mary Ann McCracken, on 9 June 1797:

> "The day before yesterday, we saw from our windows two militiamen conducted to the park by all the military in this neighbourhood, and there shot for being United Irishmen."

Amid scenes of confusion about the scaffold, erected outside the Market House in High Street, Henry Joy McCracken mounted the steps and within seconds was dangling from the hangman's rope. Illustration by John Carey. *(Historical Notices of Old Belfast and its Vicinity, Robert M Young, Belfast, 1896)*

The Joy family, including Francis Joy, founder of the *News Letter* newspaper, and Henry Joy McCracken are still commemorated in the city at Joy's Entry, off High Street. *(Author)*

McCracken had been one of those who had secretly left Belfast to meet up with his men at Roughfort, near Doagh. Defeated at Antrim, he spent the next month trying to evade capture, including periods on Slemish and Divis mountains. On 7 July he was arrested near Carrickfergus as he attempted to make his way to a boat that would have taken him to safety. After a spell in the town's gaol, he was transferred to Belfast. He was tried, found guilty, and condemned to die on the following day, Tuesday 17 July 1798. Arm in arm, McCracken and his sister walked to the Market House. Kissing Mary Ann three times, he sent her away with a friend, watching as she disappeared through the crowds. McCracken then attempted to deliver an address, but couldn't be heard above the general commotion and calmly accepted his fate. Troops, many on horseback, held back the mob as it attempted to surge forward, considerable confusion ensued and within a few minutes McCracken was swinging from the end of the rope. A boy in the crowd, John Smith, later recalled:

> "Hoarse orders were given by the officers, the troops moved about, the people murmured, a horrible confusion ensued, and in a minute or so the manly, handsome figure on which the impression of nobility was stamped, was dangling at a rope's end. The body was soon cut down, and the only favour extended to it was freedom from mutilation."

He may indeed have been cut down again in a comparatively short time, though the *News Letter* of the day reported the body hung for an hour. The

corpse was not beheaded after execution but returned to the family for burial
– leading to a desperate but intriguing attempt to revive him in his Rosemary
Lane home. His sister had summoned two doctors to come to the house who
immediately began working on the body. Mary Ann recalled years later:

> "From the moment I parted with Harry, the idea which had occurred
> to me in the morning that it might be possible to restore animation,
> took full possession of my mind, and that hope buoyed up my strength
> and supported me at the moment of parting with him. Every effort
> that art could devise was made, and at one time hopes of success were
> entertained, but the favourable symptoms disappeared, and the attempt
> was at length given up."

McCracken's body was buried in the grounds of what today is St George's
Church in High Street. Some years later, the Rev Edward May, brother-in-
law of Lord Donegall, tore up the gravestones and sold off the land. In 1902,
during demolition work at the corner of Ann Street and Church Lane, what
were believed to be the bones of Henry Joy McCracken were uncovered.
Seven years later, the remains were reburied in Clifton Street cemetery next
to his sister's grave.

The bid to revive Henry Joy McCracken was not entirely a forlorn hope.
There were several instances recorded where a hanged person was later found

Henry Joy McCracken's body was buried in the grounds of what today is St George's Church
in High Street. What are believed to be his remains were uncovered again in 1902 during
demolition work and interned in his sister's grave in Clifton Street cemetery. *(Author)*

to be alive. In 1651, a woman named Ann Greene was executed, and the body left hanging for almost half-an-hour. Cut down and placed in a coffin, she began to show signs of life. A startled soldier, perhaps as a misguided act of mercy, clubbed her with the butt of his musket. Later, as a surgeon was about to begin dissection, a small rattling sound came from her throat. She was bled and placed in a warm bed. A month later, Ann was well enough to return to her family. She died nine years later, having married and borne three children since her "execution". Another woman who survived hanging was Margaret Dickson in 1728. She was cut down after approximately an hour. Her family, taking the body for burial, stopped at an inn for refreshments on the way home. While there, a noise was heard coming from the coffin. The lid was lifted and Margaret sat up – causing panic among staff and customers! She survived another 25 years and had several children.

Another rebel believed hanged at Belfast was George Dickson, who had worked in Dickey's legal practice. Dickson apparently earned the unusual nickname of General Halt after disarming and taking prisoner five soldiers single-handedly by holding a blunderbuss to a sergeant's head and instructing him to order his troops to lay down their weapons. His prisoners on that day were said to have been among the crowd that watched his execution.

The United Irishmen's cause didn't end in 1798. Robert Emmet attempted another act of rebellion at Dublin in July 1803. He was hanged two months later. The Northern leader of that rebellion was Thomas Russell, the "man from God-knows-where". Despite evading capture initially, Russell was eventually taken prisoner in Dublin and transported to Downpatrick, County Down, where he was hanged outside the gateway of the County Gaol of Down on 21 October 1803.

* * *

SHORTLY AFTER 4.00 AM on a cold winter's morning, a terrific explosion ripped through the home of Francis Johnson, a muslin manufacturer who lived in a fine house at the top end of North Street, near Peter's Hill in Belfast. An armed gang, eight to ten strong, then rushed the front door and began firing wildly into the blackness, with the blunderbuss of Mr Johnson being the only response from inside. The commotion had raised the neighbours from their slumbers and the night watchmen, who had only passed the house a short time earlier, were already on their way back. Faced with the prospect of capture, the gang disappeared into the night.

It was, in fact, the second attack on Mr Johnson's home in seven months. Both incidents stemmed from the severe hardships being endured by Belfast weavers, many of whom were then either without work or struggling on meagre wages. In 1811 the industry, which two years before had hit a low, was booming again as the Napoleonic wars effectively eliminated foreign competition. The good times could not last forever, however, and prices began to fall again, with finished cloth only fetching two-thirds of its previous value by 1816. Even during the better times a weaver's life had been difficult, with earnings often less than 15 shillings a week out of which had to come money to pay for an assistant and materials, and sometimes the rental for a loom stand.

While some were fortunate enough to be employed by factories, the vast majority worked from hovels in the poorer areas of the town. As they were on piecework, being paid only for what they actually produced, the fall in price really stung. Although it was against the law, the weavers formed unions, or combinations as they were known, in a bid to try to force employers to take a more responsible attitude to wages. Johnson, it would appear, was particularly despised, and the union tried to stop weavers working for him altogether.

But, on 28 February 1816, a group of weavers went too far. In what was obviously a well-planned operation, the gang arrived outside the Johnson household in the early hours of the morning. Inside were sleeping the master and mistress of the house, their eight children, two maids and a manservant. The weavers began by prising off the shutters on the parlour window and pulling aside the iron bars put there to frustrate just such an attack. Raising the sash, they threw in a box filled with pitch, tar and hemp to which they had attached a ball of gunpowder – a sort of early fire bomb-cum-blast bomb. The fuse was lit and the gang retreated across the road to await the blast. In the meantime, however, the manservant had been awakened by their efforts to break in. He came down the stairs armed with a pitchfork, with which he stabbed the bomb, carrying it through the house to the kitchen door. Then he rushed upstairs again to waken his master who, armed with a fully loaded blunderbuss he kept by his bed, took up position at a front room window. From there he opened fire on the gang sheltering on the far side of the street. Seconds later the bomb exploded, blowing out the windows and doors but, deprived of its pitch, tar and hemp, doing comparatively little damage. The weavers, perhaps unaware of how little they had achieved, then rushed forward firing, with Johnson replying in kind. The fracas ended within a few seconds with no one on either side injured.

What was being described as an "atrocious outrage" could not go unpunished and five men were arrested and brought before the County Assizes in Carrickfergus that August. Three, John Doe, John Magill and

The eminent citizens of Belfast were so outraged at the attack on Francis Johnson's home that they put up a reward of £2,000, a huge sum in its day, for information leading to a successful prosecution of the culprits, and another £300 for the capture of those who may have helped them. *(Belfast Commercial Chronicle)*

DREADFUL OUTRAGE.

£2000 REWARD.

WHEREAS, on WEDNESDAY morning the 28th February, instant, about FOUR o'Clock, an Armed Party attacked the Dwelling-House of Mr. FRANCIS JOHNSON, in Peters-hill, in the Town of Belfast, and after breaking the Windows, introduced some extremely combustible preparation, which exploded with such violence, as to destroy a great part of the said House and imminently endangered the lives of the whole family, (consisting of Thirteen Persons).

Now we, whose Names are hereunto annexed, viewing with indignation and horror this infamous and malicious attempt to involve in destruction not only the Property of this respectable Gentleman and the lives of himself and Family, but those of all the neighbourhood, and anxious to bring to Condign Punishment the Perpetrators of this atrocious and diabolical outrage, do hereby promise to pay, in proportion to the sums to our names annexed, a REWARD of

TWO THOUSAND POUNDS Sterling,

to any Person or Persons, who shall, within Twelve Months from this date, discover on, and prosecute to conviction the Person or Persons, or any of them, concerned in this atrocious outrage; and we also hereby engage to pay a REWARD of

FIVE HUNDRED POUNDS,

for such Private Information as may lead to the discovery and conviction of any Person or Persons who were concerned aiding or assisting therein, and the name of the Person or Persons who shall make such private communication will be kept secret.

Application will also be made to Government for obtaining his Majesty's most gracious Pardon for any Person or Persons implicated in the above outrage, who shall give such information as may lead to conviction.

Belfast, 28th February, 1816.

Joseph Madden were accused of burglary at the Johnson home, and the other two, James Dickson and James Park, of conspiracy in the affair. All were found guilty, with Doe, Magill and Madden, despite a plea for mercy from the jury, sentenced to be hanged on 6 September 1816. Dickson and Park were given 18 month gaol terms, ordered to be publicly whipped, and bound over to keep the peace for what was a huge sum in those days of £100, with two sureties of £50 each. Both the executions and the whippings were to be carried out in Belfast, ruled the judge, as an example to others of a like mind in the town. The hangmen, however, were to be denied one of their fees. Shortly before the day of execution, the Lord Lieutenant accepted the jury's plea and changed Madden's sentence to transportation for life.

So it was that at 9.00 am on the following Friday morning only two prisoners were brought through the doors of Carrick gaol to join the procession forming up outside for the trip to Belfast. Doe and Magill were put in a chaise, a light open carriage, into which also squeezed two of the three clergymen in attendance. This allowed the huge crowd of spectators

Castle Place in 1843. It was in the widest part of the road, close to the Donegall Arms, seen on the right of the picture, that the scaffold was erected for the executions of John Doe and John Magill. (© *National Museums Northern Ireland, Collection Ulster Museum, HOYFM.WAG.3389*)

gathered outside the gaol and along the route to catch a final glimpse of the condemned men. Behind followed two carts, the first carrying the county executioner and part of his apparatus. Another executioner "from a distant county" sat in the second cart, his face covered in black crepe to hide his identity. A strong military detachment made up of the 5th Dragoon Guards and several companies of the Royal Scots formed up front and rear. At a slow and solemn pace, the convoy set off. By noon the prisoners were nearing the town, and their imminent arrival was signalled by a large detachment of troops, both on horse and foot, leaving the Belfast barracks and taking up position along the upper end of High Street to Castle Place, where the procession came to a halt. While the prisoners sat in the chaise engaged in religious devotions with the clergymen, a temporary gallows was erected. It consisted of two triangles and a cross beam, the whole about 15ft high. When it was complete, Doe and Magill were led out of the carriage and on to the platform, which was the second of the carts that had travelled from Carrick. Further devotions took place, with the prisoners praying fervently. Doe then read several passages from the New Testament "with a strong and audible voice" before giving his dying declaration, part of which read:

"As I am shortly to stand before the judgment seat of Jesus Christ, the following, in the presence of God my Saviour, are my last words, dying declaration, and true confession: I was formerly a professor of the Gospel, and united to a Church of Christ, but, forgetful of my profession, I fell from the truth, cohabited with a woman of bad character, was cut off from the Church, and thus, from step to step, was brought under the awful deserved chastenings of the Lord. I acknowledge, that although I have not been guilty of all the crimes laid to my charge on my trial, yet I have transgressed the laws of my country, and do justly merit the execution of the sentence announced upon me."

Magill declined to deliver his own declaration, but handed a paper to one of the clergymen to read. In it he denied some of the charges against him, in particular denouncing the evidence of "the approver Gray" and his wife that he had asked Gray to a meeting of muslin weavers in Mill Street. He did admit, however, his guilt on the main charge:

"I confess, however, with the deepest contrition, that I was present when the outrage was committed on Mr Johnson's house. I now see and am extremely sorry that I acted under the influence of mistaken views. I was taught to believe that Mr Johnson's family did not sleep in their own house. I had no idea of taking any lives. I now see the evil of all such combinations and outrages, though I once thought them innocent and even laudable."

With the speeches finished, the clergymen climbed down from the platform. The two executioners completed their work, placing the caps over the men's faces and tightening the nooses about their necks. Stepping down, they went to the front and quickly led away the horse and cart, leaving the men dangling. Doe, it was said, scarcely moved, while Magill had "strong convulsions" for several minutes before he too stopped moving. Surprisingly, considering the circumstances, the crowd remained placid throughout. The News Letter reported: "The whole scene was awfully impressive. A solemn stillness pervaded the multitude and the utmost order and regularity every where prevailed."

After an hour the bodies were cut down and placed in black-lined coffins provided by relatives. They were carried across the 21-arched Long Bridge (replaced by the Queen's Bridge in 1843) into County Down. Magill and Doe, both of whom left widows and young children, were buried the next afternoon in the one grave at the Knockbracken burying ground, which lies on the road from Purdysburn to Comber. Perhaps not surprisingly, given the

The solemn cortege carrying the bodies of the two weavers made its way across the Long Bridge into County Down. *(History of the Town of Belfast, George Benn, Belfast, 1823)*

desperate financial plight of their families, no headstone appears to have been erected over the grave.

The melancholy scene was re-enacted the following Friday when another procession left Carrickfergus gaol for Belfast with Park and Dickson in a cart along with the executioner. The scaffold was again erected in Castle Place, but not for a hanging but a flogging. The *News Letter* recorded:

> "Park was the first who was stripped and tied up, and received 314 lashes which the executioner inflicted with considerable effect. After he was taken down, Dickson underwent a similar punishment, and received 269 lashes. When the whole was finished, they were both re-conducted to gaol, where they are to suffer 18 months imprisonment."

CHAPTER THREE

The making of a county town

They call Belfast the Irish Liverpool; if people are for calling
names, it would be better to call it the Irish London at once
– the chief city of the kingdom, at any rate.

William Makepeace Thackeray
(Irish Sketch Book, 1842)

DESPITE A REMARKABLE GROWTH in population during the latter half of
the eighteenth century, there were still fewer than 20,000 people living
in Belfast at the time of the 1798 uprising. As the town's prosperity increased,
so did the numbers flocking to its streets. In 1811 there were 27,832 souls
in Belfast; by 1821 that number had grown to more than 37,000; and it had
leapt again to over 53,000 a decade later. The 1841 census recorded 70,447,
while the 1851 survey showed an additional 17,000 residents. Belfast had now
surpassed Carrickfergus in importance, but lacked the official recognition,
though that wasn't far away.

The majority of people living in Belfast in the mid-ninteenth century were
former farm labourers looking for a better life. In essence the country had
come to the town in the hope of finding work, a home and a decent standard of
living. Many were to be sorely disappointed. Housing had not kept pace with
demand and it was not uncommon to find three, four or even five families
sharing the one set of rooms. Squalor and misery were everywhere, as were the
ale and spirit houses that liberally supplied those who wanted to drown their
sorrows. The rapid growth in population also saw the arrival of a substantial
number of Roman Catholics in what had been predominantly a Protestant
town. Belfast had long enjoyed a reputation for religious and political
tolerance and was to the forefront in calling for Catholic emancipation. Half

the money to build the town's first Roman Catholic church, St Mary's in what is now Chapel Lane, was provided by the Protestants of the town and many were among the congregation at its opening Mass in May 1784. However, as Belfast's population grew so did sectarian frictions.

A clear picture of Belfast society at this time is provided through the writings of the Rev William Murphy O'Hanlon, who became minister at the Congregationalist Church in Upper Donegall Street late in 1849. He was shocked by the wretched living standards of the town's poor, their drinking habits, lack of morals and criminal leanings. Mr O'Hanlon was, however, a man who cared and made every effort, through a series of articles in the *Northern Whig* newspaper and later reprinted in book form, to make his more fortunate fellow citizens aware of the situation and its consequences. He wrote:

"Hulks, penal colonies, and the gallows will never ask in vain for their prey so long as society nurtures such cockatrices's dens as these. We first

The Protestants of the town provided half the money for Belfast's first Roman Catholic Church, St Mary's, Chapel Lane. As the population grew, however, so did sectarianism. *(Author)*

Rev William Murphy O'Hanlon, whose descriptions of Belfast in the mid-1800s showed the level of poverty and overcrowding in the town's back streets, had been minister of the Congregationalist Church in Upper Donegall Street. *(Author)*

Items such as this pillory, provided for the tourists to be photographed in rather than be pelted with rotten fruit and vegetables, give a nod towards Carrick's historic past. *(Author)*

make our victims, or permit them to be made in our sight, when but by an ordinary measure of exertion would suffice to anticipate the evil; and then, when full-blown, matured, and too strong for ordinary effort to manage and control, we are compelled in self-defence to bring the whole cumbrous and expensive apparatus of punishment to bear upon the evil thus engendered and nursed in our very bosom. We first warm and cherish the serpent, and when it plays the serpent we crush it; we first manufacture our criminals, or sit still while they are manufactured, and then we hang them."

Mr O'Hanlon's arrival in Belfast coincided with the end of a debate on the role of Carrickfergus as the county town of Antrim, or rather, which of its rivals might replace it in that role. The growing inadequacies of Carrick's facilities, particularly the limited accommodation in the gaol, were all too obvious. The Municipal Corporations Act (Ireland) 1840, had abolished Carrickfergus County Council from 25 October that year and the first Belfast Town Council was formed towards the end of 1842. Given Belfast's rapid growth during the preceding fifty years, it seems, certainly with hindsight, to have been the natural choice as the new county town. However, its success was not straightforward. Antrim and Ballymena were both in the running too. Initially the former seemed the favourite and it took several years of persuasion, and the formation of an influential committee of Belfast's richest and most respected citizens, to swing the case for the town. The benefits of becoming the county town were immense. Instead of Belfast having to pay for the building of its own gaol and courthouse, it merely had to contribute 20 percent of the half-million pounds they cost, with the county paying the rest – and this despite the fact that Belfast was producing more than 70 percent of the county's criminals. Likewise, the town only paid £1,200 towards the prison's annual running costs of more than £5,500 when it could have been expected to pay, based on the number of Belfast criminals being housed there, some £3,920. A report presented to the Grand Jury at the opening of the first County Antrim Assizes to be held in the newly completed courthouse on Thursday 18 July 1850, made it clear that Belfast had escaped lightly:

> "A jail and Court-house have been erected at a cost of above £480,000, Belfast only contributing about one-fifth of the expense, while, for the requirements of the borough, three-fourths of the expenditure became necessary; three-fourths of the number of committals being from Belfast, and it is idle to say, 'they are not Belfast men'. Had the borough a special jurisdiction, it would be obliged to defray the whole expenses of these offenders."

The Grand Jury threatened to introduce a Bill that would separate Belfast from the rest of County Antrim for criminal jurisdiction and fiscal purposes. Such a break did ultimately come about. Despite the arguments, the fact remained that Belfast was now the county town (it was to be another thirty-eight years, until 1888, before it received its Royal Charter and became a city) and had a fine prison and courthouse.

The former County Courthouse at Carrickfergus later became the Town Hall. *(Author)*

As already noted, Belfast was producing the vast majority of the prisoners coming before the County Court. An old gaol had existed at Howard Street in the town since 1818, with the Manor Court, the equivalent of the petty sessions, sitting in the building. The more serious criminal element was housed at Carrickfergus, which was neither practical for the constabulary nor good for Belfast's self-esteem. Following the completion of the "new House of Correction" on the Crumlin Road in the mid-1840s, two blocks of the old gaol were demolished and a proper courthouse built there. It was demolished in 1901.

The County Gaol was built from black basalt taken from quarries in the hills overlooking the town. Sandstone was imported from Scotland to add the finishing touches. The prison consisted of four wings, each with three

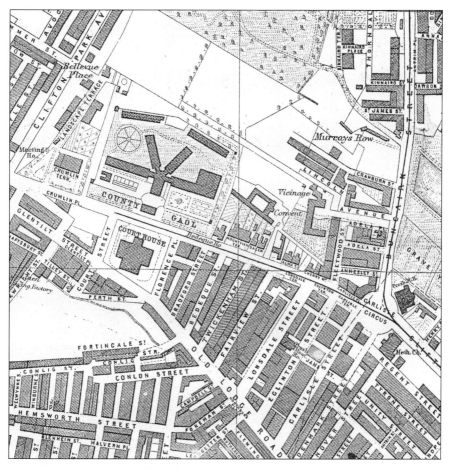

The Ordnance Survey map of Belfast in 1888 clearly shows how the then 43-year-old County Gaol's four wings radiate out from the centre. The County Courthouse, completed in 1850, stands opposite.

The administration building within the courtyard of the Gaol. *(M Johnston)*

landings, radiating out from a central hall, and was based on the then recently completed Pentonville Jail. Letters identified the wings, with A wing to the left if viewing the gaol from the Crumlin Road, D wing to the right, next to the Mater Hospital, and B and C wings spaced in between. From the upper floors, the landings look down on to what were open wells. In later years these were covered in wire mesh and partially floored in places to provide recreation areas. It was, in many ways, a traditional Victorian prison, with its design allowing warders to view all four wings from the central hallway, or Circle. Its main entrance was from the Crumlin Road, through the Governor's House-cum-gate lodge. Work on the gaol began in 1843 under the watchful eye of County Surveyor Charles Lanyon. By the summer of 1845, and only slightly behind schedule, he was able to tell the Grand Jury that the work was completed, though the gaol as yet unoccupied.

By March 1846, however, the gaol was fully operational and housing some 106 prisoners. Six were awaiting transportation, 17 serving sentences, six of whom were described as "lunatics," and the rest were awaiting trial on a variety of charges, including deserting infant children, rape, larceny, indecent exposure, passing base coins and concealing the birth of a child. Even though most were on what today would be termed remand, all inmates had to wear the prison garb, complete with wooden clogs, and both men and women

The three levels of C wing viewed from the Circle. *(M Johnston)*

had their hair cropped to the scalp. Nonetheless, having the Belfast gaol in operation was a definite bonus for all concerned, including the inmates. At the opening of the 1846 County Antrim Spring Assizes in Carrickfergus Courthouse, the Hon Justice Crampton was moved to remark:

> "I am extremely happy to hear that the new House of Correction, erected near Belfast, is answering all the purposes expected from it by those who successfully and benevolently carried out the project."

While the gaol might have been bleak and practical, the County Courthouse was considered beautiful. It is difficult to imagine today, given the high density housing which now characterises the area, but once the courthouse and gaol

The new County Antrim Courthouse, built on the outskirts of Belfast, opposite the County Gaol, was completed in 1850, from about which time this illustration dates. (© *National Museums Northern Ireland, Collection Ulster Museum, BELUM.P6.1956*)

stood in the suburbs, with the nearby mountains providing a spectacular backdrop. Work began on the Lanyon design in 1845. The main contractor was James Carlisle but it is interesting to note that the project brought together Henry McLaughlin and William Harvey as sub-contractors. Later they formed a partnership and the company still bears their name today. Atop the courthouse was the figure of Justice, her scales finely balanced. The work of Dublin sculptor Boyton Kirk, it was said to be the finest statue in the town. Inside, the Common Hall was some 47-foot square, with a large gallery on one side. Off it led the entrances to the rest of the building, which had the Crown Court occupying the west wing and the Record Court the east. A tunnel beneath the Crumlin Road connected the court to the gaol opposite, with two chambers for the prisoners to wait in, one for women and the other men. The courthouse was enlarged in 1905, with new end blocks added, recesses bricked up, and a stucco finish applied to the entire building. The amendments are said to have destroyed much of the detail of Lanyon's work.

The completion of the County Courthouse allowed the citizens of Belfast to watch the arrival of the judges at the opening of each assizes, an event carried out with great pageantry. The following account, taken from the *News Letter*, refers to the opening of the Summer Assizes of 1910. By then the courthouse held separate hearings for Belfast and the rest of the county.

"The Honourable Mr Justice Dodd travelled yesterday morning from Newcastle, where he had been staying since the conclusion of the

Dublin sculptor Boyton Kirk created the figure of Justice, atop the County Antrim Counthouse. At one time it was considered to be the finest statue in Belfast. *(News Letter)*

County Down Assizes, and arrived in Belfast at ten minutes past eleven o'clock. His Lordship was met at the city terminus of the Belfast and County Down Railway by the High Sheriff of County Antrim (Major Montgomery, D.C.) and the Under-Sheriff (Mr John R. Bristow), with the Under-Sheriff for the county of Down (Mr Hugh C. Kelly). The guard of honour consisted of fifty non-commissioned officers and men of the 3rd (Reserve) Battalion Royal Irish Rifles, under Captain A. D. N. Merriman and Lieutenant J. B. A. Drought, and a detachment of the Royal Irish Constabulary under District-Inspector Dunlop. The police band, in charge of Mr George C. Ferguson, was also in attendance. The learned Judge, accompanied by the High Sheriff and Under-Sheriff for the county of Antrim, and escorted by mounted constabulary, drove direct from the station to the County Courthouse, Crumlin Road; and the High Sheriff's equipage as it passed through the streets attracted considerable attention. The Right Honourable Mr Justice Wright, who will open the commission of Assizes for the county of the city of Belfast

The judges arrive by carriage to open the Belfast and County Antrim Summer Assizes, July 1931. *(News Letter)*

tomorrow, journeyed from Dublin by the train reaching the Great Victoria Street terminus of the Great Northern Railway at noon. His Lordship was received on the arrival platform by the High Sheriff of Belfast (Alderman George Augustus Doran, J.P.) and the Under-Sheriff (Mr James Quail). The guard of honour was composed of a detachment of the 3rd (Reserve) Battalion of the Royal Irish Rifles, and an equal number of constabulary, with band. On this occasion the carriage in which the learned Judge accompanied by the High Sheriff and Under-Sheriff, drove from the station to the Courthouse was an open landau drawn by four splendid bays. The escort consisted of mounted police. At the Courthouse, both Judges had as a guard of honour a number of men of the 1st Cheshire Regiment, and on alighting they passed into the building through a cordon of constabulary."

CHAPTER FOUR

Lords of the scaffold

Come now: the time is short,
Longing to pardon and to bless I wait.
Look up to Me, My sheep so dearly bought,
And say 'Forgive me ere it is too late'.

From a poem given to the condemned
by executioner James Berry

FINDING A VOLUNTEER TO carry out a hanging would seem a daunting prospect, yet there was rarely a shortage of candidates. Even though the post was never advertised, the Home Office received an average of five applications per week during the first half of the twentieth century from would-be executioners. Very few, however, ever got the chance to make their appearance on a scaffold.

In spite of the cloak of secrecy surrounding judicial hangings from the late nineteenth century, when it became the practice to exclude the Press and to limit what serving hangmen were permitted to say, information inevitably seeped out. The custom of recognising one particular man as the chief executioner helped focus the attentions of the newspapers on individuals. Hence many of these 'Lords of the Scaffold', such as William Marwood, who began his career in the 1870s, and his successor James Berry, became household names in their day, while Albert Pierrepoint is still remembered by many today, more than half-a-century after he last pushed a trap door lever.

Several of the early hangmen to operate in Belfast, however, not only preferred to remain nameless, but in some cases faceless as well for fear they would be identified by the baying crowds which gathered to witness their work. Military courts, operating in the wake of the failed United Irishmen uprising of 1798 condemned at least six rebels to die on the Belfast scaffold. Their executioners were likely to have been soldiers, though in the wake of the uprising it was not unknown for the military authorities to attempt to force civilians to carry out the grisly task. Dr Madden, (*Antrim and Down in '98*) quotes Dr McGee's account of how General Clavering, "an unprincipled and a merciless man," burned Randalstown after allowing two hours for plunder.

> "He proceeded then to Ballymena. One man was ordered for execution; there was no person found to act as executioner; he levied a fine of £50 on the town in consequence, the money was paid, and he then ordered another mulct of £50 to be levied if the head was not struck off and stuck on the market-house. The head was struck off, and the fine was not levied."

The two hangmen who dispatched weavers John Doe and John Magill in 1816 came from outside Belfast. One is described as the "usual executioner" from Carrickfergus. The other was "brought from a distant county; he was disguised, having his head and face covered with black crape". It was prudent for the hangman to remain as anonymous as possible. In England the condemned man, rather than the executioner, was the subject of the crowd's hatred. In Ireland it was often the other way round. Several of the latter-day hangmen felt the need to carry a gun when coming to work in the county gaols across Ireland and often travelled with police guards. By contrast, the last two executioners at Carrickfergus Gaol in the 1840s were apparently well known in the town. David Strahan, a labourer and one-time prisoner, recalled in March 1897: "The hangmen at Carrick were Alan McQuilkin and Josey Elliott and they went about openly."

The Press was inclined not to name the executioner at the early hangings in Belfast, though whether that was by choice or simply because the reporter didn't know the identity is impossible to say. At the execution of soldier Robert O'Neill at Belfast prison in 1854, the *Banner of Ulster* felt free only to say the hangman "is the same person that officiated in the counties of Armagh, Louth and Monaghan during the past few years". Even less was given away about the executioner of Daniel Ward in 1863, though his description in the *News Letter* certainly deserves mention:

> "His stature is small, he appeared to have a hump, and was veiled completely, of course… The executioner eyed the doomed man with the air of a bull-dog, and then stepped in and pinioned him without the slightest resistance."

The County Antrim Gaol at Carrickfergus. A beam protruded from above the top archway, with the criminal being pushed to his death from the doorway once the hangman's noose had been slipped over his head. Such public executions were abandoned at the gaol in 1844, however, after the hanging of an 18-year-old soldier caused public outrage.

The newspaper was led to "understand at that moment there was another candidate in the gaol for the grim office". The authorities, either due to penny-pinching or because of a genuine shortage of outside candidates, were known to sometimes appoint prisoners as executioners, their reward being an early release from the cells. Presumably the disappointed inmate in this case was obliged to complete his sentence.

By the 1870s such a casual approach to the art of hanging was drawing to an end. The Home Office, galvanised into action by a series of botched and embarrassing hangings, was seriously reviewing the procedures and would eventually bring about a uniform approach to executions. At the same time, as Belfast was about to experience, a more enlightened breed of hangman was about to enter the drama enacted on the scaffold.

William Marwood, a cobbler from Horncastle, Lincolnshire, became the main executioner in the British Isles in 1874. Chiefly employed in London, he travelled the country applying his skills and visited Belfast in 1876 to hang the coal porter John Daly. A "tall, stern and determined looking man," he is credited with inventing the 'long drop' method which greatly curtailed the suffering of those ending up on the gallows. By carefully calculating the weight of a condemned man, and gauging the strength of his neck muscles, Marwood created a table of drops whereby the length a felon fell varied. The object, generally achieved, was to break the neck rather than leave the victim to slowly die of strangulation. Marwood, who was over 50 years of age when he took on the job, is also credited with inventing the leather straps used to secure a prisoner's elbows, wrists and knees, and creating a running noose fitted with a metal ring to ensure a smoother dispatch. Among his 'clients' were five of the Invincibles involved in the Phoenix Park murders of 1883, when Thomas Henry Burke, Permanent Under-Secretary for Ireland, and Lord Frederick Cavendish, Chief Secretary of State for Ireland, were murdered in Dublin.

While Marwood earned the respect of the public, his successor, and the next hangman to come to Belfast, was often the butt of ridicule. James Berry, a former policeman and shoe salesman from Bradford, Yorkshire, had caused a sensation in November 1888 when an execution he was carrying out in Norwich Castle went terribly wrong. Berry miscalculated the drop, giving prisoner Robert Goodale too much rope, and completely pulling off his head. In 1891, this time in Liverpool, he almost did the same again, the head remaining barely attached and blood much in evidence. Such incidents were frowned upon by the authorities and seized on by the Press, who made Berry out to be a ghoul. In 1889 he came to Belfast to execute Arthur McKeown for the murder of his common-law wife. While awaiting the arrival of the condemned man, and with his 10-year-old son playing on the gallows, Berry casually gave an interview to a group of reporters, and evidently made a big impression. The *News Letter* reported:

> "Berry is not the repulsive individual which reports would lead one to believe. He is a man of medium stature, deep-chested, and strongly knit. In complexion he is sandy, and his beard and whiskers, which are closely cut, are of that peculiar coarseness, indicative of strength. His features are regular, and so far from his countenance being forbidding, were it not for a deep scar extending over a portion of the forehead, and terminating at the right eye, it would be at least pleasing if not inviting. Of his calling he seems to have a more than pardonable pride. A word dropped, a hint however trifling draws from him answers which the legal profession

Photograph of James
Berry from his book,
*My Experiences as
an Executioner. (My
Experiences as an
Executioner, James
Berry, London, 1892)*

would term speeches. With a peculiar grin, he asserts he has 'pushed off' considerably above one hundred human beings, and that the rope he was that morning using – a tried and trusty Manilla of the Government regulation type, three-quarter inch diameter – had been requisitioned on many previous occasions."

Turning on the charm, Berry – accompanied by an assistant as well as Master Berry – praised the scaffold, saying "he had never seen better in any part of the kingdom". The people of Belfast he thanked for their "intelligence and kindness". Once his work was completed, apparently without a hitch, he left the gaol for a few hours sightseeing in Belfast before catching the train to Bangor, returning from the seaside town in time to board the ferry to Fleetwood and home. Berry, who invariably carried a gun on his trips to Ireland, believed in confronting a condemned man on the morning of the execution and asking him to confess to his crime before he met his Maker. For a time he was also inclined to pass on to the prisoner, via the chaplain, a copy of a religious poem which he had come across in a newspaper. He was ordered to stop doing this after there were complaints.

The next two executions to be carried out in Belfast were performed by

Thomas Henry Scott, from Huddersfield, who was a rope maker by trade. He acted as an assistant to Berry on a number of occasions, then as second man to James Billington until 1895 when an incident ended his career in England. In December of that year he reported to Walton Prison, Liverpool, where he was to assist Billington at an execution the next day, before heading off to spend time with a prostitute who, in addition to offering her services, also robbed him of his wallet and spectacles. Scott reported the theft and its circumstances, and in response the Home Office immediately removed him from the list of approved executioners. He subsequently moved to Ireland to continue his career as a hangman, living in Dublin for a time. In 1894 he had been in Belfast to execute farmer John Gilmour, and returned seven years later to hang the down-and-out William Woods in 1901. On both occasions he appears to have carried out his task without the aid of an assistant, with no obvious detrimental results. In between these two Belfast executions he performed a number of others in different parts of Ireland, including the hangings of two men condemned at the Ulster Winter Assizes, which sat in Belfast in December 1898. County Cavan murderers Thomas Kelly and Philip King were executed respectively on 10 and 13 January 1899, at Armagh gaol. A third man sentenced to death by the same court was reprieved and later taken from Derry gaol to Mountjoy prison, Dublin, to serve his sentence. Scott, who had already hanged a man at Kilkenny prison earlier that month, was assisted on all three occasions by Batholomew Binns, who had briefly

Hangman James Berry was proud of his profession and often handed out calling cards describing himself as the "executioner". (*My Experiences as an Executioner*, James Berry, London, 1892)

To be submitted to the High Sheriff.

Memorandum of Conditions to which any Person acting as Executioner is required to conform.

1. Every person acting as executioner is required to conform to any instructions he may receive from or on behalf of the High Sheriff as to the day and hour and route for going to and leaving the place of execution.

2. He is required to report himself at the prison at which an execution it to take place, and for which he has been engaged, not later than 4 o'clock on the afternoon preceding the day of execution.

3. He is required to remain in the prison from the time of his arrival until he has completed the execution, and until permission is given him to leave.

4. During the time he remains in the prison he will be provided with lodging and maintenance.

5. By desire of the Secretary of State the supply of articles for maintenance while residing in the prison will be subject to necessary restrictions to ensure moderation, and the daily supply of alcoholic liquor to each person will be limited as under :—

1 quart of malt liquor { 1 pint at dinner,
{ 1 pint at supper.

or

¼ pint of spirit.

6. He should clearly understand that his conduct and general behaviour should be respectable, not only at the place and time of the execution, but before and subsequently; that he should avoid attracting public attention in going to or from the prison, and he is prohibited from giving to any person particulars on the subject of his duty for publication.

7. His remuneration will be £ *10* for the performance of the duty required of him, to which will be added £ *5* if his conduct and behaviour are satisfactory, during and subsequent to, the execution. These fees will not be payable until a fortnight after the execution has taken place.

8. Records will be kept of his conduct and efficiency on each occasion of his being employed, and this record will be at the disposal of any High Sheriff who may have to engage an executioner.

9. The name of any person who does not give satisfaction, or whose conduct is in any way objectionable, so as to cast discredit on himself, either in connexion with the duties or otherwise, will be removed from the list.

10. The necessary ropes, straps, pinioning apparatus, cap, &c., will be provided at the prison, and must not be removed therefrom.

11. The executioner will give such information or make such record of the occurrences as the Governor of the prison may require.

November, 1907.

z (2)18266 Pk 13 150 8/22 E & S

The authorities, embarrassed by the bad publicity generated by some of those on the approved list of hangmen, issued a number of memorandums to ensure that everyone knew what was expected from the executioners (continued on following pages). *(PRONI, D1523/2)*

4

Enclosure No. 2.

(Copy.)

Whitehall, 7th October, 1885.

SIR,

I AM directed by the Secretary of State to acquaint you that on several recent occasions his attention has been called to the proceedings, before and after an execution, of the person employed as executioner, which appear to have given rise to grave public scandal.

The Secretary of State thinks that the danger of the repetition of such occurrences would be much diminished if it could be arranged that, on the occasion of every execution, the executioner should reside in the prison while he is in the place where the execution takes place. The Secretary of State has, of course, no authority to control the movements of the executioner who is engaged and paid solely by the Sheriff, as the officer solely responsible for the carrying out of the execution; but the Secretary of State has, as you are aware, already given instructions that quarters should be provided for the executioner in the prison, whenever the Sheriff wishes him to reside there, and he thinks that it is desirable that in future, when it is known that an execution is about to take place in any prison, the Governor should be instructed at once to communicate with the Sheriff and inform him that, if he so desires, the executioner will be provided with lodging and maintenance in the prison, and that, in the opinion of the Secretary of State, he should, in engaging the executioner, make it compulsory that he should sleep there so long as he may remain in the place where the sentence is to be executed, and certainly on the night preceding the execution.

The Sheriff should, of course understand that this matter is one entirely for his discretion, but that the Secretary of State, while not wishing to interfere with his responsibility, desires him to be informed of his opinion that grave public scandals may be avoided by insisting on this as a condition in the engagement of the executioner.

I am, &c.

(Signed) GODFREY LUSHINGTON.

The Chairman of
The Prison Commissioners,
&c. &c. &c.

Continued from page 55. *(PRONI, D1523/2)*

5

Enclosure No. 3.

MEMORANDUM on the subject of EXECUTIONS.

In continuation of Memoranda issued by the Secretary of State in
October, 1885.

1. With a view to assisting the High Sheriffs in the selection and
appointment of suitable persons to carry out executions, the Secretary of
State has decided that a small list of persons who have acted in, or are
believed to be willing and competent to undertake, the office of executioner,
shall be kept at the Home Office. Records will be kept of their conduct
and efficiency on each occasion of their being employed, and the information
thus recorded will be at the disposal of any High Sheriff who may have to
engage an executioner. The name of any person who does not give satisfaction, or whose conduct is in any way objectionable, so as to cast discredit
on himself, either in connection with the duties or otherwise, will be removed
from the list.

2. When an execution is about to take place the list of names and
addresses, and the necessary information from the record kept as above,
will be sent to the Governor of the prison for the information of the High
Sheriff, and it will be left to the High Sheriff to engage one of them if he
thinks fit to do so.

3. The Committee appointed in 1886 to inquire into and to report upon
the subject of the carrying out of capital sentences were of opinion that it is.
very important and desirable that there should be an assistant to the executioner, " who might gradually acquire experience, might assist where several
" criminals were simultaneously executed, or might replace the executioner
" when he was ill, or when his presence was required in different places at the
" same time." Sanction has been obtained for the employment of such
assistants at the public expense, and the Governor may, if the High Sheriff
concurs, engage one or more persons to be present at the execution in order
to gain practical experience and to act as assistants if required under the
orders of the High Sheriff. The provisions in regard to accommodating the
executioner in the prison, and to his conduct in connection with the execution
and before and after it, will apply also to any assistant who may be so engaged.
It must, however, be clearly understood, that the engagement of assistants by
the Governor does not take away from the High Sheriff or his deputy or the
executioner appointed by him any of the responsibility attaching to the offices
they respectively fulfil.

4. Besides the suggestions contained in the letter from the Home Office,
dated 7th October, 1885, the Secretary of State thinks it desirable to express
his opinion that executioners should be made clearly to understand that their
conduct and general behaviour should be respectable not only at the place
and time of execution, but before and subsequently : that they should
avoid attracting public attention in going to or from it, and that they should
be prohibited from giving interviews for publication to any persons on the
subject of their duty. This end would be better secured by their remuneration not being payable till a fortnight after the execution, and the payment
of a part of it being made dependent upon their satisfactory behaviour.

5. The Secretary of State suggests that the persons engaged should be
required to conform to any instructions they may receive from or on behalf of
the High Sheriff as to the day and hour and route for going to and leaving the
place of execution.

6. It is suggested that the persons should be required to undertake to
report themselves at the prison at which an execution is to take place, and for
which they have been engaged, not later than 4 o'clock on the afternoon
preceding the day of execution ; also that they should remain in the prison
from the time of their arrival until they have completed the execution and
until permission is given them to leave.

A 3.

Continued from page 55. *(PRONI, D1523/2)*

6

7. With a view to carrying out the objects referred to in paragraphs 1 and 2 as to the record to be kept of the conduct and efficiency of the person or persons employed as executioner or assistant, High Sheriffs are requested to be good enough to make a report to the Home Office in regard to the manner in which the duty has been performed on each occasion. Reports as to their conduct, character, and efficiency will also be made by the Governor, &c. These reports will be recorded at the Home Office, and the information they afford will (as stated in paragraph 1) be placed at the disposal of any High Sheriff who has to appoint an executioner.

8. Straps, pinioning apparatus, &c., and ropes will be put at the disposal of the High Sheriff with and on the same conditions as the rest of the apparatus referred to in the memorandum issued in 1885. They will be available at the prison.

9. A memorandum of " Conditions to which any person acting as " executioner is required to conform," having reference to the terms of his engagement and his personal conduct ; also a memorandum of " Instructions " for carrying out the details of an execution " have been furnished to the Governors of prisons for the assistance of the High Sheriff if he thinks it desirable to adopt them, when he becomes responsible for the carrying out of an execution.

10. The Secretary of State wishes it to be clearly understood that the suggestions made in this memorandum are not intended in any way to interfere with or diminish the responsibility of the High Sheriff attaching to him by Statute, and in particular that, from the moment when the condemned prisoner is handed over to him, the executioner acts entirely under the Sheriff's orders, and that the Sheriff is alone responsible for his conduct and for his treatment of the prisoner, e.g., in allowing or refusing to allow him to make any statement, or to speak with the Chaplain.

Home Office, Whitehall, December, 1891.

N.B.—As soon as the High Sheriff has fixed a date for an execution he should officially inform the Home Office.

Continued from page 55. *(PRONI, D1523/2)*

succeeded Marwood as the principal State executioner until he was removed because, as one prison Governor put it, he "had no idea how to do his work properly". Shortly after the Woods execution in Belfast the Irish authorities also sacked Scott as hangman after learning the details of why he had been dismissed by the Home Office.

In 1909 the most famous name among modern executioners, Pierrepoint, appeared in Belfast for the first time in person. The occasion was the hanging of Richard Justin, one of 19 executions Harry Pierrepoint carried out that year. In his black-bound Execution Book, in which he noted the birth of his children, the addresses of assistant executioners, and cures for cow coughs as well as the details of the men he hanged, he recorded his expenses for the trip: £1 11s 3d was his fare to Belfast, plus a shilling for the cab. Harry was the first of a dynasty which was to last almost to the end of hanging itself in Britain. Another Yorkshireman, he applied for the job of hangman when he was just 25, and assisted at his first execution in 1901. He apparently enjoyed his work and, unlike his companions, was inclined to celebrate afterwards. It was common practice for him to head for the pub immediately he came out of a prison after completing an execution. Sometimes his drinking binges lasted up to a week. It seems likely, judging by comments made by subsequent family members who took up the profession, that he was also fond of a drink or two before an execution. An unusual feature of Harry Pierrepoint's term as executioner was his habit of placing the noose around the prisoner's neck before pulling on the white hood. It was generally more usual to do it the other way round, so saving the condemned man from the feel of the rope on his skin and reducing the likelihood of visible injuries to the neck. Harry resigned as hangman in 1914, by which time his older brother, Thomas, was well established in the 'family business'.

But before the Pierrepoint name was to reappear in Belfast, another famous, and tragic, executioner was to be called to the city. John Ellis was coming towards the end of his hanging career, which had spanned almost a quarter of a century, when he accepted the call to execute child killer Simon McGeown in 1922. From a respectable Rochdale family, he incurred the wrath of his father when he applied for the post but, despite threats of being disowned, pressed on, being accepted on to the list of approved hangmen in 1901. He was a man singularly unsuited to such a profession and suffered from a nervous condition that at times caused a form of virtual stage fright. Nonetheless, his career progressed and in 1907 he was competent enough to be selected to act as 'number one' executioner for the first time. Over the next two decades he was to be associated with some of the most infamous executions of the century, including the hanging of American murderer Dr Hawley Harvey Crippen in 1910. Six years later it was Sir Roger Casement, who had been convicted of treason, who was to feel Ellis's rope about his neck. Casement, who had enjoyed a highly successful career in the Foreign Office, had spent the early years of the First World War in Germany, where he attempted to establish an Irish Brigade by recruiting prisoners of war to fight the British. Later, after negotiating German support for the planned 1916 uprising, he travelled to Ireland by U-Boat, but was arrested virtually as he set foot ashore. Convicted at the Old Bailey of treason, he was hanged by Ellis at Pentonville on 3 August 1916.

The Casement affair was by no means the end of Ellis's connection with Irish politics, and he returned time and again to execute those condemned to death as a result of the violence that consumed Ireland following the end of the war and partition. In 1923 another celebrated case came Ellis's way. Edith Thompson, along with her young lover Frederick Bywaters, was condemned to be hanged for murdering her husband. The execution caused a public outcry, which was later inflamed by reports of the poor physical and mental state of the woman in her final days and hours. All those involved in the hanging, including Ellis, were badly affected by the experience, and he resigned as hangman the following year, having carried out in excess of 200 killings. Within a few months he attempted suicide, but only managed to wound himself with the gun. In September 1932, after taking a few drinks, he succeeded in taking his own life by slitting his throat with a razor.

The next hangman to utilise the Crumlin Road scaffold was William Willis, who had acted as assistant to Ellis at the hanging of McGeown. His return, this time as the 'number one', came two years later for the execution of Michael Pratley in 1924. Although he acted as the chief executioner in a handful of hangings in Great Britain, including that of Mrs Thompson's lover Bywaters, his career was primarily confined to that of assistant hangman. By the time he retired from the gallows in 1926, he had been in attendance at more than 100 hangings over a 20-year period.

Another Pierrepoint appeared in Belfast in 1928, this time in the form of Thomas, brother of the aforementioned Harry. Thomas Pierrepoint, however, was a different kind of character, and was to become by far Belfast's most regular hangman, monopolising executions in the city up to the Second World War. His first victim was Smiley, followed in 1930 by Cushnan, 1931 Dornan, 1932 Cullens, 1933 Courtney and Williams in 1942. Thomas is said to have sucked sweets as he prepared the prisoners for the drop and clearly tackled his task in a detached and workmanlike manner. He is estimated to have carried out more than 300 hangings in total in a career that continued up until 1946, when he retired aged 73. Harry's son Albert Pierrepoint began his apprenticeship as hangman by assisting his uncle Thomas in Dublin in 1931. Albert, who is arguably the best remembered of the modern hangmen, never got to practice his craft in Northern Ireland as chief executioner. He numbered Ruth Ellis and Derek Bentley, the latter posthumously reprieved, among his victims. While in Great Britain the Home Office selected assistants, in Northern Ireland it was left to the High Sheriff to arrange. For the most part, the authorities were willing to accept Thomas' suggestion that Albert come along as his assistant. It was this pairing which hanged Harold Courtney in 1933. The correspondence between Pierrepoint and the Under-Sheriff of Armagh, Valentine Wilson, reveals the secrecy involved in employing an executioner, and the security measures taken. Notable in the letter below is the query about any other executions that week. The hangmen were inclined to accept all jobs that came their way, even if the dates clashed, in the belief that at least one of the condemned would be reprieved.

The letter to Pierrepoint, dated 20 March 1933, reads:

Dear sir,

Harold Courtney was at Armagh Assizes on Saturday last convicted of the murder of Minnie Reid, and was sentenced to death, and to be hanged at Belfast Prison on Friday, 7th April, 1933.

Will you please wire me on the enclosed form if you can act as executioner on this occasion. Wire Yes or No on the enclosed form, and sign your name "Legal".

In addition to sending me the wire you will please write me confirming your wire to me, and further stating if you have any other executions during that week beginning 3rd April, and if any, where?

If I engage you as executioner also state in your letter what route you will travel to Belfast. You would have to travel not later than Wednesday, 5th April, arriving in Belfast not later than Thursday, 6th April.

Send me wire at once, and write also to me tomorrow, Tuesday.

Yours faithfully,
Under-Sheriff, Co Armagh

Thomas wrote back and as usual suggested Albert as assistant executioner. His nephew was then new to the official list of trained hangmen and would have been unknown to Mr Wilson. Nonetheless, the Under-Sheriff agreed to Pierrepoint's request, but with the rider: "Of course, if through any unforeseen accident or illness on your part you cannot attend, I would prefer to have another person on the List who has experience of carrying out executions acting as the principal, but in any case with your nephew as assistant". Belfast Police Commissioner FA Britten was also told of the hangmen's arrangements and asked:

I would feel grateful if you would arrange to have a constable in plain clothes on arrival of Heysham Boat on Thursday, 6th April, to see these two men to the Gaol at Belfast, and also to see them depart from Belfast on the Heysham Boat on Friday night, 7th April.

The arrival and departure of the Executioner and his Assistant should be kept strictly private.

31st March, 1933.

Dear Sir,

Harold Courtney, a Prisoner, is to be executed in Belfast Prison on Friday, 7th April 1933, for the murder of Minnie Reid.

I have appointed Thomas W. Pierrepoint as Executioner, with Albert Pierrepoint as his Assistant. They will travel via Heysham, and arrive in Belfast on Thursday morning, 6th April. I would feel grateful if you would arrange to have a Constable in plain clothes on arrival of Heysham Boat on Thursday, 6th April, to see these two men to the Gaol at Belfast, and also to see them depart from Belfast on the Heysham Boat on Friday night, 7th April.

The arrival and departure of the Executioner and his Assistant should be kept strictly private.

Thanking you in anticipation.

Yours faithfully,

Under-sheriff, Co. Armagh

F. A. Britten Esq., O.B.E.
Commissioner of Police,
Police Office,
Chichester St.,
BELFAST.

Any further communications on the subject of this letter should be addressed to:—
"THE COMMISSIONER, R. U. C. BELFAST,"
and the following number quoted:-
....
Communications should not be addressed to individuals by name.
Telephone No. 3981.

COMMISSIONER'S OFFICE,

ROYAL ULSTER CONSTABULARY,

BELFAST,

3rd April 1933.

PERSONAL.

Sir,
———

I have received your letter of 31st ult, with reference to the execution of Harold Courtney at Belfast Gaol on 7th inst. The necessary arrangements will be made with regard to the arrival and departure of the executioners.

I am, Sir,
Your obedient servant,

F. a. Britten

COMMISSIONER.

Valentine Wilson, Esq.,
48 Church Street,
Portadown,
Co. Armagh.

While confidentiality was sought at all levels to ensure the safe arrival and departure of the executioners, the RUC was still asked to be on hand to escort the men to and from the gaol. *(PRONI, D1523/2)*

The Commissioner, of course, obliged. Meanwhile, Mr Wilson was making arrangements with Pierrepoint in the event of a reprieve. It was not unknown for a prankster, or anti-hanging activist, to try to sabotage proceedings:

"If there should be a reprieve, and I have to wire you, will you kindly note that my wire will be signed "Valentine Wilson" with the word "Seal" immediately after. Remember, the word "Seal" must be on the telegram to you to show that it has my authority."

In the event it was not to be. A telegram dispatched following a Cabinet meeting at Stormont on 5 April, and signed by the Minister of Home Affairs, gave the execution the green light:

"Case of Harold Courtney has received careful consideration. Cabinet of Northern Ireland have failed to discover any grounds which would justify them in advising his Grace the Governor to interfere with the due course of the law. His Grace has accordingly decided that the law must take its course."

The Under-Sheriff later put in a bill to the Ministry of Home Affairs for £29 14s 0d, including £5 2s 0d incurred by himself for hiring a car to get him to and from Crumlin Road Gaol because there was a rail strike at the time. The authorities declined to meet this extra expense. The rest of the bill broke down as follows:

	£	s	d
Executioner's fee	12	–	–
Fare from Bradford to Belfast	2	15	–
Cabs		9	–
Subsistence allowance		10	–
Assistant executioner's fee	4	–	–
Fare from Manchester to Belfast	2	10	–
Cabs		8	–
Subsistence allowance		10	–
Portadown Times A/c for printing	1	10	–

Pierrepoint senior received an advance of £10, with another £2 being sent on later if it was decided "his conduct and behaviour are satisfactory,

Part-time executioner and publican Harry Allen, who cut a fine dash in his three-piece suit and bow tie, carried out the last two hangings in Northern Ireland. *(Press Association)*

during and subsequent to, the execution". Not a great deal of money by any standards. The printing bill was for the production of declaration forms, to be nailed outside the prison, initially announcing the execution was to take place and later that it had been carried out according to the law.

Albert Pierrepoint, who ran a pub when not operating a scaffold, became the first-choice executioner in Britain following his uncle's retirement, but never returned to the province. He resigned in February 1956, ending the Pierrepoint's 55-year reign. Albert later claimed to have carried out a staggering 550 hangings, including large numbers of war criminals – five times his father's total.

Following the Pierrepoints' exit from the scene, two men – Les Stewart and Harry Allen – were jointly made the 'number one' executioners. It was the latter that brought hangings in Belfast to an end when he came to Northern Ireland twice in 1961. Allen, from Manchester and also a publican, had spent many years in Pierrepoint's shadow. He was already considered one of the most senior assistants at least a decade before his big chance came and had performed a number of executions as the chief man. Syd Dernley, an assistant hangman who worked on occasions with Allen during the 1940s, had mixed feelings about him. On one occasion the pair, along with another assistant also called Harry Allen, came together for a double execution at Wandsworth Prison. Dernley recalled:

> "The Manchester Harry Allen seemed a cheerful type, if a little flamboyant; I could scarcely believe the bow tie! He was friendly enough, in a condescending way that announced that he was the senior assistant and we were mere newcomers."

Stewart and Allen carried out the last two executions in Britain: Peter Anthony Allen was hanged at Walton Prison, Liverpool, by Stewart, and Gwynne Owen Evans by Allen at Strangeways Prison, Manchester. Both were carried out on 13 August 1964.

CHAPTER FIVE

Until you are dead

I think it is quick, certain and humane. I think it is the fastest and quickest in the world bar nothing. It is quicker than shooting, and cleaner.

**Executioner Albert Pierrepoint
on the merits of hanging**

ALTHOUGH THE ULTIMATE OBJECTIVE was always the same – to "hang by the neck until dead" – the ritual and methods of execution have varied over the centuries. At one time it was the preserve of the courts to determine where, when and how a condemned man died, with the finer details added by the individual hangmen. Judges sometimes favoured taking a culprit to the scene of his crime or even to his own front door to meet his fate, the object in the latter case being to set an example to the prisoner's friends and relatives. In such instances, a temporary scaffold was erected at the chosen place of execution or a convenient tree employed.

By the time executions became routine in Belfast, however, the pattern had become well established if not entirely formalised. Following the abandonment of public hangings, the Home Office formally outlined how a criminal convicted of a capital offence was to meet his end, while still leaving the High Sheriff as the responsible party. In 1885 a series of documents was issued from Whitehall that, although added to and occasionally altered, provided the basis for executions for the next eighty years. The Governor dispensed copies of these papers to the relevant County Sheriff once an inmate had been convicted of a capital offence. What the documents basically did was tell the Sheriff, as if he were in any doubt, that he was "solely responsible for carrying into effect

H.M. Prison.

19

SIR,

In obedience to instructions I beg leave to acquaint you that prisoner

has been received into my custody under sentence of death, and to forward, for your information, copies of the under-mentioned Memoranda, &c., in reference to the carrying out of executions :

Enclosure No. 1.—Memorandum of instructions on the subject of executions issued by the Secretary of State in 1885.

Enclosure No. 2.—Letter dated 7th October 1885 from the Secretary of State to the Prison Commissioners.

Enclosure No. 3.—Further memorandum on the subject of executions issued by the Secretary of State, and dated December 1891.

Enclosure No. 4.—Memorandum of conditions to which it is suggested that any person acting as executioner should be required to conform. (Two loose copies of this memorandum are enclosed for transmission to the person whom you may engage as executioner in case you should require him to conform to the conditions therein laid down— one copy may be retained by him for guidance and the other returned to you with a signed acknowledgment thereon that he will conform to the conditions.)

Enclosure No. 5.—List of candidates reported as competent for the office of executioner.

Enclosure No. 6.—A copy of the rules made by the Secretary of State, pursuant to the provisions of the Capital Punishment Amendment Act, 1868, for regulating the execution of capital sentences.

I am further to inform you that I have in my keeping a " Memorandum of instructions for carrying out the details of an execution," also a " Table of Drops." These instructions will be available for the guidance of the executioner while in the prison, should you desire him to adopt them, and if you wish it, I will forward these documents to you for your personal perusal, but I am directed to request that you will kindly return them to me in accordance with the note thereon.

I am, Sir,

Your obedient Servant,

Rw4 Shephensor
Governor.

Under
To the High Sheriff

No. 275.

℔ (E)18162 Pk 12 100 7/22 E & S

A

Enclosures sent to the Sheriff, or Under-Sheriff, outlining his duties, which included organising an executioner and ensuring the scaffold was up to standard (continued on following pages). *(PRONI, D1523/2)*

3

Enclosure No. 1.

MEMORANDUM of INSTRUCTIONS on the subject of EXECUTIONS, issued
by the SECRETARY OF STATE in 1885.

The Sheriff being solely responsible for carrying into effect the sentence
of death, and for this purpose, or for any purpose relating thereto, having
by statute the control over the prisons and the officers thereof, whenever
a Governor receives a prisoner under sentence of death he is forthwith to
inform the Sheriff of the fact, and to specify what means exist at the time in
the prison for carrying out the sentence.

The Governor will invite the Sheriff to inspect the apparatus and to test
its operation ; so as to satisfy himself of its efficiency in every respect.

He is also to inquire of the Sheriff whether he desires any works to be
done in the prison, either to improve the apparatus or to facilitate the
carrying out of the execution, and if the Sheriff answers in the affirmative
the Governor is to inform him that the responsibility rests with him, and that
he is at liberty, and it is his duty, to select and employ at his discretion
proper workmen, and to direct them to carry out such works as he thinks
necessary, but that the Prison Commissioners will offer all requisite facilities
and will, if requested in due time, place at his disposal all such labour
and materials as they have at their command free of cost (unless otherwise
notified to him).

8

Enclosure No. 6.

RULES made by HIS MAJESTY'S PRINCIPAL SECRETARY OF STATE for
the HOME DEPARTMENT, pursuant to the provisions of the Capital Punishment Amendment Act, 1868, for regulating the execution of CAPITAL
SENTENCES.

1. For the sake of uniformity it is recommended that Executions should
   take place in the week following the third Sunday after the day on
   which the sentence is passed, on any week day but Monday, and
   at 8 a.m.

2. The mode of execution and the ceremonial attending it to be the
   same as heretofore in use.

3. A Public Notice, under the hands of the Sheriff and the Governor of
   the Prison, of the date and hour appointed for the execution to
   be posted on the Prison Gate not less than twelve hours before the
   execution, and to remain until the inquest has been held.

4. The Bell of the Prison, or if arrangements can be made for that
   purpose, the Bell of the Parish or other neighbouring Church, to
   be tolled for 15 minutes after the execution.

5. The person or persons engaged to carry out the execution should
   be required to report themselves at the Prison not later than
   4 o'clock on the afternoon preceding the execution, and to remain
   in the Prison from the time of their arrival until they have
   completed the execution and until permission is given them
   to leave.

Approved by the
   Secretary of State,
     Whitehall,
       5th June, 1902.

Continued from pervious page. *(PRONI, D1523/2)*

the sentence of death, and for this purpose, or for any purpose relating thereto, having by statute the control over the prisons and the officers thereof". He was invited to inspect the gallows and prison facilities with a view to making any alterations he felt necessary. At least part of an executioner's pay, he was advised, should be retained for a couple of weeks after the hanging to ensure their good behaviour before, during and after the event. On a more general note, the Sheriff was asked to ensure that the execution took place during the week following the third Sunday after the day on which the sentence was passed, on any weekday bar a Monday; that a public notice, stating the date and time of execution, be posted on the prison gate; and that the prison bell be tolled for fifteen minutes after the hanging.

In practice, the prison trade staff at Crumlin Road tested the equipment before the executioner and his assistant arrived, which was normally on the afternoon prior to the hanging. The hangmen, after depositing their overnight bags in their room, would be taken to the scaffold. At this point they would usually stop on the way to peer at the condemned man through the peephole in the cell door to assess his build. For this purpose the warders had their charge sitting at the table playing cards or some other game, with either his back or side view to the door. The alternative was to take the condemned man out for some fresh air in the exercise yard, allowing the executioner to view him from a distance. In either case, it was felt important that the prisoner was not aware that he was being assessed for the grim business the next morning.

Once in the execution room, there was a short delay while the executioners waited until the prisoner had been taken from the cell, usually to the chapel or exercise yard, so there was no danger of him overhearing the preparations. The rigging of the apparatus was comparatively simple. All the necessary equipment was supplied by the Home Office and came in two black wooden boxes, one larger than the other. From the smaller box, which also included pulley blocks, the executioner removed a length of chain. With the aid of a stepladder, this was attached to the crossbeam. The larger box contained two ropes, linen hoods, straps, copper wire, thread and chalk. One of the ropes (often one was brand new while the other had already been used several times) was shackled to the end of the chain, having first been marked with the required length of drop. Dividing the man's weight in pounds by 1,000, and converting the answer into feet and inches, was how the drop was calculated. A 'Table of Drops' was provided, of course, but at the end of the day it was at the executioner's discretion whether he went for the recommended distance or added or subtracted inches according to his assessment of the prisoner's build and allowing for age. By adjusting the chain, the mark on the rope was

The Crumlin Road Gaol's execution box contained everything the visiting hangman required to carry out his job. *(Irish News)*

set at head height. The rope's slack was then taken up in a series of loops, which were held together with thread from the box, leaving the noose hanging at the right height to slip over the condemned man's head. The noose itself was covered in leather to minimize the amount of visible damage caused to the neck, and worked by running through a brass eye. After being attached it was held in place by a rubber or leather washer.

Next the hangmen, using a tape measure, calculated exactly the centre of the trap doors, marking the point with a chalked 'T'. Unless the prisoner was stopped on exactly the right spot, he would end up swinging back and forth when dropped. When in the right position, however, the body hung virtually motionless. A 'dummy' run with a sand bag acting as the body was then carried out, often in front of the prison Governor, engineering officer and the High Sheriff or his representative. Everyone then left the execution room, the door being locked behind them. The sand bag was left hanging overnight to ensure the rope was fully stretched. The hangmen then retired to their room for tea, followed by what must have seemed a long and tense evening playing cards, reading or chatting.

Early next morning the hangmen returned to the scaffold to remove the sand bag, reset the trap doors, and check the preparations of the previous

Northern Ireland Spring Assizes, 1933.

County of Armagh — To Wit

By the Lords Justices of Assize for the Circuit of Northern Ireland at a General Assizes, Session of Oyer and Terminer, and General Gaol Delivery held at Armagh in and for said County on Monday the Thirteenth day of March, 1933.

Whereas, Harold Courtney late of Church Street, Dungannon in the County of Tyrone was, at the said Assizes in due form of Law, indicted, tried and convicted that between the 26th day of July, 1932, and the 4th day of August, 1932, at Derryane in the County of Armagh aforesaid he feloniously wilfully and of his malice aforethought did kill and murder one Minnie Reid against the Peace of our Lord the King his Crown and Dignity, and thereupon Judgment was given by the Court that the said Harold Courtney be taken from the Bar of the Court where he now stands to the Prison whence he last came and that on Friday the Seventh day of April in the Year of our Lord One thousand nine hundred and thirty three he be taken to the common place of execution in the Prison in which he shall be then confined, and then and there hanged by the neck till he be dead and that his body be buried within the precincts of the Prison in which the aforesaid judgment of death shall be executed upon him.

And it was ordered by the Court that execution of the said Judgment be done upon him in manner and form aforesaid on Friday the Seventh day of April, One thousand nine hundred and thirty three.

These are therefore in His Majesty's name strictly to charge and command you the Sheriff of the said County of Armagh in whose custody in His Majesty's Gaol at Belfast the said Harold Courtney now remains that you repair to the said Gaol and thereout take the body of the said Harold Courtney and that you cause execution of the Judgment aforesaid to be done upon the said Harold Courtney in manner and form as above set forth on Friday the Seventh day of April, One thousand nine hundred and thirty three, and for your so doing this shall be your sufficient Warrant.

Sealed with my Seal of Office and dated this First day of April One thousand nine hundred and thirty three.

By the Court

_____
Clerk of the Crown and Peace for the said County of Armagh

To
The Sheriff of the County of Armagh
and his Assistants.

A warrant, issued by the court to the Sheriff and his assistants, gave them the legal right to have a prisoner, in this case Harold Courtney, "hanged by the neck until he be dead". *(PRONI, D1523/2)*

I, PATRICK E. O'FLAHERTY, the Surgeon of H.M. Prison at Belfast, hereby Certify that I this day examined the body of Harold Courtney, on whom Judgment of death was this day executed in the Prison, Belfast, and that on examination I found that the said Harold Courtney was dead.

Dated this 7th April, 1933.

P.E. O'Flaherty

We, the undersigned, declare that Judgment of death was this day executed on Harold Courtney in the Prison, Belfast, in our presence.

Dated this 7th April, 1933.

Valentine Welsh ?

Under Sheriff of County Armagh.

Ross Stephenson

Governor of H.M. Prison, Belfast.

Within minutes of an execution, notices were placed on the prison door confirming for the crowds gathered outside that the sentence of death had been carried out. (*PRONI, D1523/2*) evening. With any adjustments carried out, and the noose again tied up at head height, the 'number one' and his assistant retired to await the call. A few minutes before 8.00 am, the executioners were conducted back to the condemned cell by a warder. The official party would already be in position to one side of the scaffold. This group, although sometimes varying in size, always included the prison Governor or his deputy, the medical officer, and the High Sheriff or his representative. At the stroke of 8.00 am, both men entered the condemned cell and quickly walked up to the prisoner, who was stripped to his shirt with his neck bared. He would be deliberately seated with his back to the entrance, usually engaged in prayers with the chaplain. Tapping him on the shoulder to get him to stand, the chief executioner bound his arms behind his back. Turning, he led the way on to the scaffold, the prisoner following with the two prison warders close at hand and the assistant and chaplain bringing up the rear. The 'number one' stopped the man on the trap doors, positioning him on the chalked 'T' marked earlier. As he pulled the white hood over the man's head, followed by the rope, the assistant bound the legs with a leather strap. The metal eye of the noose was placed under the jaw, slightly to the left, with the intention of breaking the neck between the first, second or third cervical vertebrae. The spinal cord was also likely to be destroyed, either being crushed or torn from the brain stem. If a prisoner was likely to struggle, planks were placed across the trap doors so that the warders could stand either side to restrain him. When both hangmen had stepped clear, the principal executioner pushed over the lever, and the trap doors fell, launching the prisoner to his doom. The whole operation, from entering the cell until the freeing of the trap doors, certainly took less than half-a-minute and sometimes barely ten seconds.

The assistant hangman and prison doctor then descended, through a small trap door, into the room below where the body was hanging. The medical officer checked for signs of life, including listening for a heart beat (which it has been claimed could continue for up to twenty minutes after the drop). Both men returned to the scaffold, which was then cleared and the room locked so the body could hang undisturbed for an hour. At 9.00 am, the executioners returned and, using the pulley blocks from the smaller box, lifted the corpse up, loosened the noose, and placed the body in a coffin ready to be inspected by the inquest jury. A small block of wood was placed under the dead man's head before the viewing. Apart from making their report to the Governor, that effectively completed the executioners' job and they would normally have been free to leave the prison before 10.00 am.

CHAPTER SIX

The killing machine

I do not know whether a murderer is more likely to repent and make a good end on the gallows a few weeks after his trial or in the prison infirmary thirty years later.

CS Lewis

FOR THE FIRST HALF-CENTURY of executions at the new County Gaol on the Crumlin Road, the gallows were individually constructed for each of the condemned, and dismantled again once the deed was done. It was a time-consuming business, and other inmates of the prison were often used as unpaid labourers. The first hangings were public affairs, with the scaffold, parts of which were borrowed from Carrick gaol, erected against the prison wall but within view of the crowds that gathered in the adjoining roads and open fields. While in later years every effort was made to make the prisoner's journey to the gallows as short and, hopefully, as painless as possible, little effort was made to do so in the early days. Soldier Robert Henry O'Neill, the first man to face that harrowing walk in 1854, had to make his way along the full length of D wing and up several flights of stone stairs to the 'Press Room' adjacent to the gallows platform. He was spared climbing further steps on to the scaffold, and the crowd was deprived of seeing him dangling from the rope once he had fallen through the trap doors.

The arrangements for the hanging of Daniel Ward, in 1863, were very similar. However, in 1868 the law was changed, with the public excluded from witnessing what had been a popular spectator sport. Consequently, with the sentencing of John Daly to be hanged in 1876, a new location had to be found for the gallows, which were to take the best part of a week to construct. The *News Letter* reported:

> "It was placed at the entrance to what was formerly known as the debtors' prison, at the north end of the jail. The scaffold was in the form of an oblong platform, having a trap-door in the centre. This door did not, as in ordinary constructions of the kind, open into two parts, but opened and fell in one connected piece, a 56lb weight being attached to it by means of a cord, which passed through several small pulleys running along the lower portion of the platform to prevent it from springing back and coming in contact with the body. The platform was about 12ft wide by 16ft or 17ft long, resting on six strong supports, and was about 10ft from the ground. At each side were uprights supporting a thick cross beam, from which hung a new rope, about 1in thick, having a running noose attached."

The passageway under the scaffold served as a viewing room, with the body lowered into a black-painted deal coffin that was then set on a stand for inspection by the inquest jury.

The one-piece trap door was an unusual contrivance even at a time when all prisons designed their own scaffolds. In 1885, a former Royal Engineers' officer, Lieutenant Colonel Alten Beamish, designed for the Home Office what was to become the standard gallows. The hangman James Berry suggested a modification which called for a "slope or a level gangway" to replace steps up to the platform. This he claims was first employed in April 1890, at Kirkdale Gaol, Liverpool. His memory, however, let him down for as the *News Letter* reported of the 1889 visit to Belfast of the "Bradford celebrity" for the execution of Arthur McKeown:

> "There was nothing peculiar in the scaffold, the mechanical portion was on the exact plan of all others erected in this country. There was, however, this difference taken as a whole; the culprit was not asked to ascend a staircase, the platform being on a level with the corridor."

On this occasion the scaffold was constructed at the end of D wing, next to the modern Mater Hospital. It was totally enclosed, with a temporary staircase also built to allow it to be entered from outside the main prison as well as through a doorway in the corridor. In order to allow a sufficient drop, a three-foot trench had to be dug in the ground below the double trap doors, with the exposed clay sprinkled with sawdust. The condemned cell was now

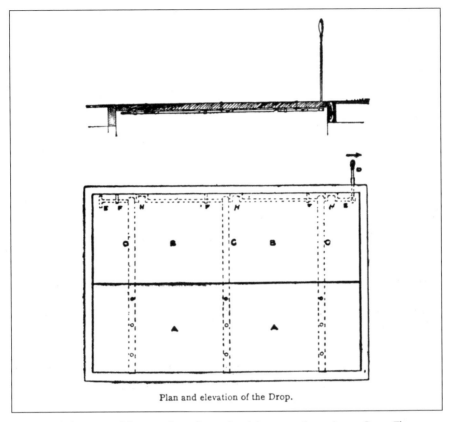

Plan and elevation of the Drop.

A plan and elevation of the trap doors from a book by executioner James Berry. The lever, marked D, was pushed, rather than pulled as is commonly believed, forcing bar E to the left. This released the crossbars, marked O, and ensured both sections of the trap fell together. A Royal Engineers officer had designed it in 1885. (*My Experiences as an Executioner, James Berry, London, 1892*)

only some 30 feet away from the entrance to the gallows, a vast improvement on earlier executions. John Gilmour, hanged in 1894, died in the same spot and most likely on the same gallows, for it had become normal custom to dismantle the scaffold and store it for further use, rather than building a totally fresh one.

By the time William Woods came to breath his last in Crumlin Road Gaol in 1901, however, the authorities had decided to make the scaffold a permanent fixture. The new execution chamber was in fact a stone extension of C Wing, again on the hospital side, but further away from the Crumlin Road. At the time it was described as a "substantial apartment, entered from the corridor of the prison, with roughly plastered walls". The trap doors themselves made up a considerable portion of the floor space. A smaller trap door in the floor lifted to reveal stairs that took the assistant executioner and doctor down into

SCALE SHOWING THE STRIKING FORCE OF FALLING BODIES AT DIFFERENT DISTANCES.

Distance Falling in Feet — Zero	8 Stone	9 Stone	10 Stone	11 Stone	12 Stone	13 Stone	14 Stone	15 Stone	16 Stone	17 Stone	18 Stone	19 Stone
	Cw. Qr. lb.	Cw. Qr. lb.	Cw. Qr. lb.	Cw. Qr. lb.	Cw. Qr. lb.	Cw. Qr. lb.	Cw. Qr. lb.	Cw. Qr. lb.	Cw. Qr. lb.	Cw. Qr. lb.	Cw. Qr. lb.	Cw. Qr. lb.
1 Ft.	8 0 0	9 0 0	10 0 0	11 0 0	12 0 0	13 0 0	14 0 0	15 0 0	16 0 0	17 0 0	18 0 0	19 0 0
2 ,,	11 1 15	12 2 23	14 0 14	15 2 4	16 3 22	18 1 12	19 3 2	21 0 21	22 2 11	24 0 1	25 1 19	26 3 9
3 ,,	13 3 16	15 2 15	17 1 14	19 0 12	20 3 11	22 2 9	24 1 8	26 0 7	27 3 5	29 2 4	31 1 2	33 0 1
4 ,,	16 0 0	18 0 0	20 0 0	22 0 0	24 0 0	26 0 0	28 0 0	30 0 0	32 0 0	34 0 0	36 0 0	40 0 0
5 ,,	17 2 11	19 3 5	22 0 0	24 0 22	26 1 16	28 2 11	30 3 5	33 0 0	35 0 22	37 0 16	39 2 11	41 3 15
6 ,,	19 2 11	22 0 5	24 2 0	26 3 22	29 1 16	31 3 11	34 1 5	36 3 0	39 0 22	41 2 16	44 0 11	46 2 5
7 ,,	21 0 22	23 3 11	26 2 0	29 0 16	31 3 5	34 1 22	37 0 11	39 3 0	42 1 16	45 0 5	47 2 22	50 1 11
8 ,,	22 2 22	25 2 4	28 1 14	31 0 23	34 0 5	36 3 15	39 2 25	42 2 7	45 1 16	48 0 26	51 0 8	53 3 18
9 ,,	24 0 11	27 0 12	30 0 14	33 0 23	36 0 16	39 0 18	42 0 19	45 0 21	48 0 22	51 0 23	54 0 25	57 0 26
10 ,,	25 1 5	28 1 23	31 2 14	34 3 4	37 3 22	41 0 12	44 1 2	47 1 21	50 2 11	53 3 1	56 3 19	60 0 9

The hangmen calculated a suitable falling distance using a 'Table of Drops'. As a rule of thumb, they looked for a striking force of 24 cwt, but could add or subtract inches according to how muscular they felt the condemned man's neck was, and allowing for his age and general health. *(My Experiences as an Executioner, James Berry, London, 1892)*

another bare room in which the body hung for an hour after the drop. These rooms, virtually unaltered, remained the place of execution within the gaol up until the abolition of the death penalty.

Next to the execution chamber was the condemned cell where the prisoner and his warder escorts waited out his last days. The rooms were connected by an entrance, hidden from the prisoner's view, which was revealed only seconds before the execution was to take place. It must have come as a shock to many a prisoner to realise that he had been living and sleeping barely a dozen steps away from the place he was to meet his end. The condemned cell itself was twice as big as a normal cell but was otherwise unremarkable. It was sparsely furnished with a bed, table and three chairs. Unusually for Crumlin Road Gaol, where 'slopping out' remained the norm, it was equipped with washing and toilet facilities. The prison also supplied a radio, writing paper, pens and a kettle for making tea. The last item caused some warders a wry smile. A condemned man was not allowed a belt or shoelaces, or indeed anything that could conceivably be used in a suicide attempt, yet the prison supplied a three-foot long kettle cable ideal for a bid to rob the hangman of his fee.

A condemned man was excluded from the normal routine of the prison. He was allowed, within reason, as many visits from friends and relatives as he liked. He was seen by the prison doctor every day and a clergyman was free to

A cupboard in the condemned cell hid the door into the execution chamber – a noose still hangs for the benefit of visitors. *(M Johnston)*

come and go as he pleased. According to the Home Office, in evidence to the Royal Commission on capital punishment in 1949, "amenities such as cards, chess, dominoes, etc, are provided in the cell, and the officers are encouraged to – and in fact invariably do – join the prisoner in these games". Newspapers and books were also provided, while "a pint of beer or stout is supplied daily on request, and 10 cigarettes or half an ounce of pipe tobacco are allowed unless there are medical reasons to the contrary". The only "medical reasons" that would have stopped such a modest comfort, presumably, would be the fear the cigarettes would kill the prisoner before the State had a chance to!

Under no circumstances were other inmates allowed to meet, let alone associate, with the condemned man for fear they would help him commit suicide. On a pleasant day, for example, the prisoner might request to go for a walk in the gaol's garden, which was usually granted. First, however, all other inmates were either locked in their cells or in the dining area. So as to cause as little disruption as possible, most trips out were either during breakfast, lunch or evening meal times, or after lock-up. The death watch warders would ring a bell to let the other staff know the prisoner was on his way, and he would be escorted to and from his destination as quickly and directly as possible. All meals were cooked especially for the prisoner by an officer in the prison hospital's kitchens, again for fear inmates would poison the food in order to

Confidential.

[*By order of the Secretary of State, this document is to be treated as most strictly confidential, and, in any case, when a copy is supplied to a Sheriff he is requested to return it to the Prison Governor from whom he received it.*]

Memorandum of Instructions for carrying out the details of an Execution.

1. The apparatus for the execution may be tested in the following manner :—

   The working of the scaffold should be first tested without any weight. Then a bag of sand of the same weight as the culprit should be attached to the rope, and so adjusted as to allow the bag a drop equal to, or rather more than, that which the culprit shall receive, so that the rope may be stretched with a force of about 1,000 foot-pounds. The working of the apparatus under these conditions should then be tested. The bag must be of the approved pattern, with a thick and well-padded neck, so as to prevent any injury to the rope and leather. As the gutta-percha round the thimble of the execution ropes hardens in cold weather, care should be taken to have it warmed and manipulated immediately before the bag is tested.

2. After the completion of this testing the scaffold and all appliances should be locked up, and the key kept by the Governor or other responsible officer until the morning of the execution; but the bag of sand should remain suspended all the night preceding the execution, so as to take the stretch out of the rope.

3. The executioner and any persons appointed to assist in the operation should make themselves thoroughly acquainted with the working of the apparatus.

4. The lever should be fixed so as to prevent any accident while the preliminary details are being carried out.

5. Death by hanging ought to result from dislocation of the neck. The length of the drop is determined according to the weight of the culprit.

6. The required length of drop is regulated as follows :—

   At the end of the rope which forms the noose the executioner should see that 13 inches from the centre of the ring are marked off by a line painted round the rope; this is to be a fixed quantity, which, with the stretching of this portion of the rope, and the lengthening of the neck and body of the culprit, will represent the average depth of the head and circumference of the neck after constriction.

   About two hours before the execution the bag of sand should be raised out of the pit, and be allowed another drop so as to completely stretch the rope. Then while the bag of sand is still suspended, the executioner should measure off from the painted line on the rope the required length of drop, and should make a chalk mark on the rope at the end of this length. A piece of copper wire fastened to the chain should now be stretched down the rope till it reaches the chalk mark, and should be cut off there so that the cut end of the copper wire shall terminate at the upper end of the measured length of drop. The bag of sand should be then raised from the pit, and disconnected from the rope. The chain should now be so adjusted at the bracket that the lower end of the copper wire shall reach to the same level from the floor of the scaffold as the height of the prisoner. The known height of the prisoner can be readily measured on the scaffold by a graduated rule of six feet long. When the chain has been raised to the proper height the cotter must be securely fixed through the bracket and chain. The executioner should now make a chalk mark on the floor of the scaffold, in a plumb-line with the chain, where the prisoner should stand.

   These details should be carried out as soon as possible after 6 o'clock, so as to allow the rope time to regain a portion of its elasticity before the execution, and, if possible, the gutta percha on the rope should be again warmed.

x (2)18161 Pk 12 100 7,22 B & S

Home Office instructions underlining how it expected an executioner to carry out his task. It is unlikely, given they had been trained in the use of the apparatus before making it onto the approved list of hangmen, that there was ever much call to refer to it (continued overleaf). *(PRONI, D1523/2)*

2

7. The copper wire should now be detached, and after allowing sufficient amount of rope for the easy adjustment of the noose, the slack of the rope should be fastened to the chain above the level of the head of the culprit with a pack-thread. The pack-thread should be just strong enough to support the rope without breaking.

8. When all the preparations are completed the scaffold should remain in charge of a responsible officer while the executioner goes to the pinioning room.

9. The pinioning apparatus should be dexterously applied in some room or place convenient to the scaffold. When the culprit is pinioned and his neck is bared he should be at once conducted to the scaffold.

10. On reaching the gallows the duty of the executioner should be as follows :—

    (1) Place the culprit *exactly* under the part of the beam to which the rope is attached.

    (2) Strap the culprit's legs tightly.

    (3) Put on the white linen cap.

    (4) Put on the rope round the neck quite tightly (with the cap between the rope and the neck), the metal eye being directed forwards, and placed in front of the angle of the lower jaw, so that with the constriction of the neck it may come underneath the chin. The noose should be kept tight by means of a stiff leather washer, or an india-rubber washer, or a wedge.

    (5) Go *quickly* to the lever and let down the trap doors.

11. The culprit should hang one hour, and then the body should be *carefully* raised from the pit. The rope should be removed from the neck, and also the straps from the body. In laying out the body for the inquest the head should be raised three inches by placing a small piece of wood under it.

December 1901.

Continued from previous page. (PRONI, D1523/2)

give the condemned man what they would see as an 'easy way out'. As a result his meals were of a generally higher standard and any special requests were normally honoured. All food was consumed in the condemned cell.

Warders were encouraged to strike up a relationship with the prisoner in the hope it would take some of the tension out of the situation. Six prison officers made up the death watch team. They worked in pairs and followed a complicated shift pattern. It was a traumatic time for all concerned and several reportedly had to be treated for nervous conditions in the aftermath of an execution. It is doubtful if anyone involved in the process escaped emotionally unscathed. Indeed, a hanging had a sobering affect on the entire prison population. On the actual day of execution the rest of the prison population would be given their breakfasts in the cells, where they remained until the early afternoon and the completion of the entire process. The gaol was

The wooden staircase used by the doctor to examine the hanged man, in the room below the trapdoors of Crumlin Road Gaol's execution chamber. *(M Johnston)*

unusually quiet, like a Sunday. Even the terrible clanging which accompanied the opening and closing of the heavy metal doors virtually ceased, as there was little movement within the prison. As the hour of execution approached, the silence and tension intensified. On the stroke of 8.00 am, however, the gaol erupted as inmates demonstrated their anger and disgust at what was going on in their midst by banging chamber pots, metal cups and plates on floors and cell doors. After three or four minutes, the gaol again lapsed into an uneasy silence.

Following the abandonment of public executions, legislation required an inquest to be held within the gaol so a verdict of lawful killing could be recorded. This normally sat at 10.00 am in the Governor's office and was generally, though not always, a formality. Before the sitting the inquest jury was offered the opportunity to view the body. Officials giving evidence were urged to be as vague as possible in answering questions put to them. Indeed, in January 1925 the Home Office advised:

"Any reference to the manner in which an execution has been carried out should be confined to as few words as possible, eg, 'It was carried out expeditiously and without a hitch'. No record should be taken as to the number of seconds, and, if pressed for details of this kind, the Governor should say he cannot give them as he did not time the proceedings, but 'a very short interval elapsed' or some general expression of opinion to the same effect."

Governors were, however, permitted to own up to any undue delay or hitch and give a full account of the problem.

All that remained to be done was the burial, with the grave already having been dug the previous day by the gaol's trade staff. A prison chaplain conducted the funeral service, which was generally attended by the Governor and a handful of warders. In the early days of the gaol's history the coffin would have been filled with quicklime to accelerate decomposition. This practice was later abandoned. Officially the graves were to be unmarked, however notches, and in some cases sets of initials and even whole names were carved into the garden wall, indicating where individuals were buried. The location of others could only be guessed at. To make it more difficult to mark the burial site, the trade staff fenced off the area around a grave until the grass had a chance to recover.

SECTION TWO

A Chronological Account

CHAPTER SEVEN

Public entertainment

O Let me ask you what shall become of you or I if we sleep the sleep of death.

Written by Daniel Ward while awaiting execution

Execution of Robert Henry O'Neill

21 June 1854

PRIVATE ROBERT HENRY O'NEILL holds the dubious distinction of being the first prisoner of Crumlin Road Gaol to have been executed. His crime was the shooting dead of Robert Brown, his corporal, on 22 August 1853, though whether it was a deliberate act or an unfortunate accident is still open to debate. What is certain, however, is that the events of the previous three days were enough to sway the jury into believing he had a motive.

Described by some as a sectarian crime, it seems more likely that O'Neill, a Roman Catholic, was a victim of military bullying and had, at least in the opinion of the jury, simply 'snapped'. Born in a public house in Belfast's Berry Street, he had had a hard upbringing. Abandoned by his mother while still an infant, O'Neill and his sister were more or less left to their own devices by their father, who died while they were still young. At the age of 13 he went to live with an uncle in Hercules Street (later to be redeveloped into Royal Avenue) but it was not a happy home. In April 1853, at the age of 19, he enlisted in the army but almost immediately regretted it and went into hiding. Two months

Born in a public house in Berry Street, O'Neill had a hard upbringing, spending his teenage years with an uncle in Hercules Street, seen here being demolished in 1879 as part of the redevelopment that produced Royal Avenue. (© *National Museums Northern Ireland, Collection Ulster Museum, 10/21/216)*

later he was turned in by another youth and forced to move to the barracks where, no doubt, his reception would not have been a warm one.

The unfortunate sequence of events which was to lead him to the gallows began on Saturday, 20 August 1853, when Corporal Brown, a Londoner, ordered O'Neill and another soldier to clean windows at the barracks – a task he failed to do. The same order was given the following day, at which point the corporal told O'Neill he intended reporting him to his officer. That resulted in the private being given three days' confinement to barracks and extra drill, beginning on the Monday. During that day the discontented soldier let several of his colleagues know of his anger towards the corporal and even, it was later alleged, threatened to kill him. At 8.30 pm he returned to his billet after the punishment drill, placing his musket in the rack. The corporal was already in the room, warming himself by the fire. A short time later he sat himself down at a table and began writing a letter, while the other soldiers in the room lay on their beds reading or chatting. O'Neill returned to the rack and lifted down the musket and began cleaning it with a rag. A minute later the room reverberated to the crack of the firearm and the corporal lay across the table mortally wounded. He was carried to the hospital where he died two hours

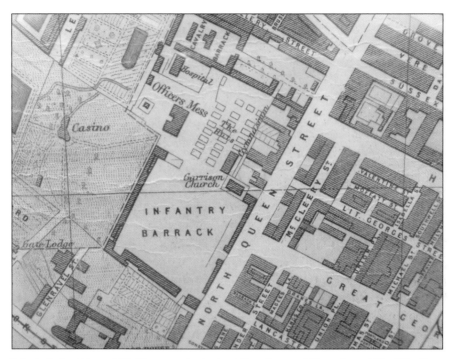

Private Robert Henry O'Neill was a reluctant soldier who would have found life difficult at the infantry barracks after initially going AWOL. This Ordnance Survey map from 1888 shows the barracks in Belfast occupied the site where the Westlink now crosses North Queen Street and was coincidently close to the Crumlin Road.

later. Corporal Brown was just one day short of his twentieth birthday. A postmortem later revealed that the ball had struck the corporal between the eyes, passed out the left cheek, and into his chest about two inches below the collar bone, ending up in the left side of his back. O'Neill, who had thrown down the weapon and tried to make a run for it, was caught in the parade ground and placed in the guardroom.

At his trial during the Spring Assizes of March 1854, it transpired that O'Neill had borrowed the weapon from another soldier, who had been admitted to hospital less than three hours before the shooting. It was claimed that he had been unaware the musket was loaded. Before a packed courthouse, which included many soldiers from the 12th Regiment to which both the victim and the accused belonged, the defence argued with some justification that there was a conspiracy against O'Neill. The prisoner, in particular, accused Sergeant John Hardy of lying about an alleged confession on the morning following the shooting. He had not reported the alleged guardroom incident until just four days before the trial began. It was also asserted that,

Victoria Barrack, in North Queen Street, had been a military base from the late eighteenth century. The buildings to the left were built in 1883, while to the right stands the older part of the barracks. *(Courtesy of the National Library of Ireland)*

judging from the direction the ball entered the corporal's body, it must have ricocheted off a shelf first. That, it was said, proved that O'Neill had had no intention to harm anyone.

The jury, however, was unconvinced and returned a guilty verdict, reportedly causing the judge, Mr Sergeant Howley, to burst into tears! Sentencing was deferred until the next day when his Lordship donned the black cap while O'Neill sobbed in the dock:

> "It only remains for me to pass upon you the sentence of the law, which is that you, Robert Henry O'Neill shall be taken from the place where you now stand back to the jail, that thence, on Friday, the 5th day of May, you shall be taken to the place of common execution – the gallows – and that you shall be hanged by the neck until you be dead. Your body shall be buried within the precincts of the jail, and may the Lord have mercy on your soul."

This time it was too much for both O'Neill and the judge. As his Lordship leaned forward, his head in his hands "under feelings of the deepest and most tender emotion," the prisoner fainted and had to be carried out of court by the warders. The drama was by no means over. Two days before the execution

was due to take place it was postponed until 14 May to allow legal arguments
to continue. News of the late, and as it turned out temporary, reprieve did
not reach everyone and on the morning of 5 May crowds began gathering
outside the gaol to await the execution. By lunchtime there was an estimated
3,000 people and the police had to be called in to disperse them. The *Banner
of Ulster* newspaper reported:

> "The mass of the 'unwashed', unwilling to believe those who told them
> that the execution would not take place, resolutely kept their ground till
> two o'clock, and not a few were satisfied to occupy their positions till
> a late hour in the evening. The state of feeling among the lower orders
> of society, indicated by the circumstance referred to, furnishes its own
> melancholy comment."

The date of execution was put back again, firstly to 22 May, then 14
June. O'Neill was sent to Dublin on 29 May for a hearing at the Court of
Queen's Bench on 1 June, which considered a challenge that there had been
irregularities in the case regarding the jury panel and the judge's failure to ask
the prisoner if he had anything to say before judgment was passed. Two weeks
later, the court finally ruled against O'Neill and he arrived back in Belfast on
16 June looking thinner and even more haggard than before. He was met at
the train station by a prison van that took him back to Crumlin Road Gaol,
accompanied by a police escort.

O'Neill ate well on his last night despite lapsing into tearful bouts of
depression. He spent time with his priests before retiring to bed, fully clothed,
for several hours. At midnight he rose again and spent the rest of the night
in prayer. "I will have long enough to sleep till the Day of Judgment," he told
a prison official who encouraged him to rest longer. At 6.30 am the clergy
returned and Mass was said in a room adjoining the condemned cell. An
aunt and another female relative were allowed a brief, and final visit, before
O'Neill returned to his religious preparations. Outside, meanwhile, police
reinforcements had been drafted in, including 110 men from County Antrim
and a further 30 from County Down, in a bid to control the huge crowd that
was rapidly gathering and which was determined that neither the law nor
the heavy rain that day would stop them having a good time. The *Banner of
Ulster* reported:

> "Shortly after ten o'clock the brickfields, streets, roads and fields and
> ditches adjoining, were covered by a multitude of not less than eight
> thousand persons, comprising a large number of boys, principally of

O'Neill's victim, Corporal Robert Brown, was buried in Shankill Cemetery, Belfast. *(Author)*

that class who may be seen in the Police Court hall and docks, women of disreputable appearance, and the dregs of society generally – a really respectable man not appearing within the range of our vision."

Detachments of the 62nd and 68th Foot regiments arrived at the gaol shortly before 11.00 am, forming up inside the railings, while a troop of the Queen's Dragoon Guards forced the mob back into the fields and away from the road. At 11.30 am O'Neill, dressed in army fatigues and accompanied by three priests, was led from the condemned cell in the southern wing of the prison, and up four flights of stairs into a small room off a landing. At 12.10 pm he was brought out, with his hands already bound and the white cap placed on his head. As he walked on to the scaffold he came into public view for the first time and an almighty roar went up from what was now estimated as a 15,000-strong crowd. The executioner, apparently a "man of considerable experience" according to the News Letter report of the day, quickly placed him on the trap door and adjusted the rope about his neck. Stepping back he pushed the lever and O'Neill disappeared from view. However, "the neck did not appear to have been broken, and a convulsive struggle continued for two minutes and a-half". The mob, no longer able to see the spectacle, fell silent. After hanging for 45 minutes, the body was taken down. In the presence of the two relatives who had earlier visited him, the corpse was stripped, dressed in a shroud and placed in a coffin to be carried to the rear of the gaol for burial.

By an odd coincidence, the last person to be publicly hanged at Carrickfergus, in 1844, was also a soldier, John Cordery, who murdered his sergeant on returning to barracks after a night of heavy drinking.

The compassionate Rev William Murphy O'Hanlon, whose articles in the *Northern Whig* newspaper had highlighted a lack of morality among Belfast's poor, returned to England in October 1854, only four months after O'Neill's execution. No doubt he would have been saddened, though not entirely surprised, by the young man's demise given his description of the barracks area:

> "Let me first direct your eye to some of the purlieus of North Queen-street. Every one must have noticed the close affinity existing between intemperance and the grosser forms of sensuality; and this quarter exhibits, in immediate juxtaposition, facilities for the indulgence of both these classes of vice. How far the idle, and, in general, dissolute habits of the soldier life in barracks may have to do specially with the case, I must leave your readers to judge. But it is a fact that no region of the town seems to be more fully furnished with the elements and means of immorality than this."

* * *

Execution of Daniel Ward
8 April 1863

SHAW'S BRIDGE, ON THE fringes of south Belfast, today plays host to thousands of visitors who picnic in the adjoining car park or enjoy quiet walks along the towpath by the River Lagan. But the bridge's narrow roadway was formerly a busy thoroughfare that linked counties Antrim and Down and, in 1862, a magnet for people who wanted to see for themselves the scene of a murder which had sent ripples of disgust and shock through the townsfolk of Belfast and beyond.

It was on 10 May 1862, that the spilling of blood for the pathetic sum of just £2 shattered the tranquility of what was then the heart of the countryside. The victim, Charles Wilgar, was a carpenter by trade who was working away from his Ballylesson home. During the week he would stay with an uncle,

Daniel Ward was initially imprisoned in Downpatrick gaol after his arrest but later brought to Belfast for trial. *(Author)*

William Wright, on what is now the Upper Malone Road, going home after work on a Saturday to be with his parents, who lived some three miles away. On this particular weekend he had tea at the Wright's as usual and then set off in the company of Daniel Ward, a fellow carpenter who had called at the house earlier in the day. When Wilgar failed to arrive home his parents raised the alarm. Ward, when approached by the family, said he had left Wilgar early on, after the young man had said he was going to meet his brother returning from Belfast.

The police at Newtownbreda were called in and soon established that a watch belonging to Wilgar had been pawned in Lisburn on the same night he had disappeared. Ward, the natural suspect, his wife and mother-in-law were then arrested on suspicion and lodged in Downpatrick gaol. On Wednesday, 14 May, a search of the riverbank turned up signs of a struggle and a boat was sent for. Within a few hours the river gave up Wilgar's body. Stewart McClieve, one of those who had fished it out, later recalled, "There was blood all round his head. The blood streamed from his head when he was taken out of the water." The river in the immediate vicinity was then dragged and a stone tied up in a handkerchief recovered.

When the case against Ward came to trial, the demand for seats in the County Courthouse, Belfast, was such that tickets had to be issued. A series of witnesses gave evidence that they had seen Wilgar and Ward leave the

Shaw's Bridge, today a haven of tranquillity in south Belfast, was the scene of a murder that shocked the rural community. *(Author)*

house together about 6.30 pm on the Saturday and walk towards Shaw's Bridge. Others told how they had noticed the prisoner by himself a short time later, walking away from the river. Later still, Ward was seen in Lisburn, with several people placing him in the pawnshop where Wilgar's watch was found. One of the most damning pieces of evidence came not from a witness but a second watch. This had been given to Wilgar by his uncle, just before he left the house, so he in turn could pass it on to his brother. The transaction had been completed out of Ward's sight, and the watch was still in the dead man's pocket when the body was recovered. It had stopped at a quarter past seven, giving a possible time when the body had entered the river. After a three-day hearing, the jury returned a guilty verdict and the judge, Baron Deasy, pronounced sentence of death. Visibly affected by the moment, he donned the black cap:

> "It now only remains for me to terminate the painful scene by announcing in formal terms that sentence which the law requires the judge to pronounce, and compels the executive ministers of justice to carry into effect, and that sentence is that you, Daniel Ward, be taken from the dock in which you now stand to the jail in which you have hitherto been

confined, and that from that you be taken on Wednesday, the 8th day of April, to the place of public execution, and there be hanged by the neck till you are dead, and that your body be buried within the precincts of the jail within which you shall have been last confined after conviction. And may the great God who has created you have mercy upon your immortal soul."

Ward, who had shown no emotion throughout, remained resolute. Catching his forelock with his right hand, he bowed to the bench, turned, and smartly left the dock. Throughout his trial Ward had maintained his innocence. Once found guilty, however, he immediately dropped the pretence and wrote out a full confession, which was published after his death. It left no doubt as to his guilt and spelt out clearly just how desperate a man he was:

"I, Daniel Ward, now a prisoner in the County of Antrim Jail, Belfast, and under sentence of death for the murder of Charles Wilgar, on the 10th of May last, in the presence of Almighty God, before whom I must soon stand, do make the following confession, and declare every portion of it to be strictly true:

On the evening of the 9th May I was in Belfast seeking for employment at any work I could obtain but did not succeed. I left Belfast between four and five o'clock that evening, and, during my walk home I thought of, as the last remedy, robbing or murdering someone in order to get money. My mind did not settle at that time on anyone in particular but I felt no act whatever would prevent me from obtaining it.

Before reaching home, I called at William Wright's to ask him if he could give me a job, for I was idle. So far, as to murdering Charles Wilgar in particular had not taken possession of my mind, nor any other, if I could get money in any other way. On the next morning, May the 10th, I went to Belfast. On going, I sat upon a heap of stones, thinking what to do; I took up a stone, and put it into my pocket-handkerchief. I left Belfast between three and four o'clock that evening. On this evening, also, I went to William Wright's and waited till Wright and Wilgar returned from work.

My object in waiting in Wright's was till it was dusk, that I might obtain by some means what I wanted, and had not up till this time settled my mind in taking the life of Charles Wilgar. After tea in Wright's, I started, with Charles Wilgar, towards home, and I do not think it was five minutes before the act that I determined to take his watch or life. I knew he had a watch. We came to a narrow path – he went on before me. I took then the stone which was in my handkerchief out of my pocket and gave him a blow. He fell, but did not speak. He was rising, I think, on his hands and feet. I then gave him the second blow – took his watch from him, and put him into the water. The plunge appeared to revive him, for I saw him swimming across the Lagan, and thought he would get out at the other side. I then threw the stone and handkerchief into the water, and went to Lisburn and pawned the watch for two pounds – and when, on Monday evening, I heard he was missing, I knew he was drowned."

Ward was obviously not a popular man. Indeed, a petition begging for a reprieve apparently received little support for fear it might actually succeed and result in him eventually returning to the neighbourhood. There was a widespread suspicion that he may have been involved in other violent incidents. Ward himself appears to have referred to these allegations in another part of his confession when he said, "I also solemnly declare, before God, that I never injured so as to take away the life of any other man, woman, or child."

Ward's last few days in gaol were marked with the same outward composure he had displayed throughout his imprisonment and trial. Although two warders were with him constantly at nights, with another posted outside the door in case assistance was needed, only the latter precaution was considered necessary during the day. On the Monday of his last week his parents visited him, and "sobbed as if their hearts would break" as they parted. The following day his mother and an aunt came to the prison and again the tears flowed, though not on the part of Ward who, bar a momentary lapse in the presence of his Episcopalian clergyman, the Rev Charles Allen, remained steadfastly dry-eyed. His wife, however, failed to make an appearance. She had left for Scotland on the day the judgment was announced, leaving the couple's child with its grandmother.

On Wednesday 8 April 1863, he rose early after a fairly sound night's sleep. At 6.00 am the Rev Allen joined him for almost two hours of devotions. Like many a condemned man before and after him, Ward had turned to God in his blackest hour, making his last four months, "the happiest days of my life". At 7.45 am, a solemn procession formed up outside the condemned cell. With Ward, cap in hand, in the centre, the clergyman to his left and a warder to the right, he began his final journey. Behind came several warders, the High Sheriff, the Under Sheriff, and the Governor of the gaol walking in pairs. A posse of journalists brought up the rear. Slowly they made their way along the passageway and up the stairs, stopping in the room that led out to the scaffold. Further prayers were said before the hangman appeared some ten minutes after 8.00 am and pinioned Ward's arms behind his back. Still accompanied by the Rev Allen and a warder, he was led out on to the scaffold which, as in the previous execution, had been erected at the front of the gaol so as to be fully visible to the public. Ward, already dressed in his shroud, remained calm throughout, and even lent his head to one side to make it easier for the executioner to attach the rope. As the hangman retreated, Ward made one last appeal to heaven, "O Lord Jesus, be merciful to my soul. God pardon my sins for the sake of the Redeemer, and bless all my fellow creatures". At this point the bolt was withdrawn and he plunged through the gap. The crowd, estimated to be up to 9,000 strong, let out a shriek, breaking the silence that had befallen it on the prisoner's appearance. Lacking a shoe, which had came off when a foot caught the edge of the drop, the body hung for about an hour before being taken down and placed in a coffin. Only the officials who had made up the death procession were present when burial took place in a plot close to O'Neill's last resting place.

CHAPTER EIGHT

A private affair

To prevent such frightful spectacles in a Christian country and all the incalculable evils they engender, I would have the last sentence of the law executed with comparative privacy within the prison walls.

Charles Dickens after witnessing a public execution

Execution of John Daly

26 April 1876

THE RESIDENTS OF BATHURST Court, a tiny row of houses off Belfast's Durham Street, awoke on the morning of 15 September 1875, to a sight that was to chill them to the bone. Lying on the pavement was the naked body of a woman, her corpse a bloodied mess. A crowd soon gathered to gawp, but no one was able to put a name to the poor unfortunate. Eventually a little girl, drawn by all the commotion, identified the victim as a charwoman called Margaret Whitley, who had lived close by. The search for her killer could now start in earnest, and it wasn't long before a picture started to emerge. Within hours it had been established that the dead woman was a relative of the wife of a coal porter named John Daly, who lived in Durham Street. It was also soon learnt that she had spent the previous evening at the Daly household and that there had been some sort of fracas. Daly was arrested as he went about his work and his house searched. Before the day was out the police had gathered enough evidence to guarantee Daly an appointment with the hangman.

John Daly, 47 at the time of his execution, was born to a farming family that worked a smallholding close to Dungannon. One of three children, he lost his father while still very young. His older brother was also to lose his life tragically early in an accident at a local coal pit. Daly took on the responsibility for the running of the farm and managed to support the rest of the family. However, a dispute over the land led to a family rift, and Daly left, moving to Belfast in 1863. He found work labouring on the quayside and soon fell in with a mill girl named Mary Anne Whitley, a niece of the murdered woman. It was she, and the demon drink, that were to be the cause of his downfall. Both Daly and his wife became alcoholics, living in squalor to afford their habit. Their two rooms in the house in Durham Street, which they shared with their 12-year-old daughter and blind infant son, were virtually devoid of furnishings. The bed was a pile of straw spread on the floor and covered with a cloth. A table and stool were the only other pieces of furniture. Everything else that had once adorned the house had been pawned for cash for drink. Mrs Daly frequently indulged her addiction with her maiden aunt, Margaret Whitley, also an alcoholic. This, it would appear, rankled with Daly.

On the Monday before the murder, in what was probably not an untypical occurrence, a row had erupted in the Daly home that resulted in him throwing his wife out. The following day he arrived home from work early to find she had returned to the house and once again he turned on her, this time using violence to force her out. Daly then gave his daughter the family clock to pawn before heading back to work. However, the pawnbroker's cash was spent by Mrs Daly and Whitley on alcohol – no doubt the purpose Daly had had in mind for himself – and when he arrived home he found both of them drunk in the house. His wife, however, was not so intoxicated that she did not see the danger and fled, leaving her aunt lying on the makeshift bed. Daly, outraged, picked up the stool and struck the woman in the presence of his daughter, who then fled the house. Unperturbed, Daly continued his savage attack, inflicting wounds to the head, face, arms and abdomen. When the frenzy passed, he realised he would have to dispose of the body. Just how he managed that is a matter for conjecture, for Daly never confessed to the murder. It would appear that, in order to avoid leaving a trail of blood, he had first stripped away the bloodied garments then wrapped the corpse in items of clothing belonging to his wife. Then, sometime during the night, he attached a rope to the body and dragged it from his house to the spot where it was found. Possibly using the same method and rope, which was later found by the police in the house, he dragged her clothes to a drain a little distance away. Daly then set off for his work as usual. Later, when he was arrested, the

Durham Street, where murderer John Daly lived, and the alleyways and streets off it were among the poorest in the city by the late nineteenth century. This image of Beatty's Entry, close to where the body of Daly's victim, Margaret Whitley was found, clearly illustrates the deprivation that still existed some 30 years later. (© *National Museums Northern Ireland, Collection Ulster Museum, BELUM.Y8525*)

police checked for bloodstains on his body, but could find none. A search of the house, however, provided ample evidence of violence. The bed and walls were liberally splattered with blood, while the floor "seemed as if blood had been actually spilled out of a vessel on it".

The two-day trial could only have one conclusion and Daly became the next resident of Crumlin Road Gaol's condemned cell. He threw himself into the spiritual preparations for his death, guided by the Roman Catholic chaplain and the Sisters of Mercy. Though on the eve of his death he was to praise both the Governor and his warders for their care and attention, he virtually refused to speak with them throughout his imprisonment. On the Monday before the execution his mother paid him a last emotional visit during which both parties wept openly. The meeting was ended early, with the Governor promising she could return the next day. Later still, Daly's wife, who "by her want of prudence and propriety hastened the degradation and ruin of her husband" called with him. She was the last relative to see him, for

Daly sent a message to his mother asking her to go home to Dungannon and not remain in Belfast for the execution.

Meanwhile, the finishing touches to the scaffold were being completed. Since Ward's hanging, the law had been altered and executions were no longer to take place in public. As a consequence, the gallows were built at the north end of the gaol, outside what had once been known as the debtors' prison. On Tuesday, his last night, clergy and two Sisters of Mercy joined Daly for his religious devotions. After a few hours sleep, he was awakened by a warder at 5.30 am and celebrated Mass in his cell at 6.00 am. Two hours later, at the appointed time, the executioner entered the cell and pinioned his arms after the Under Sheriff had read the execution warrant in the presence of the prison Governor. The formalities completed, Daly, dressed in prison clothing and physically shaking with fear, began the short walk to the scaffold. Alongside him was the priest, reading prayers, with the executioner behind. Once at the gallows, it was all over in seconds, the hangman swiftly adjusting the white cap and rope before stepping back to release the trap door. The drop of approximately eight feet was apparently sufficient to cause instant death.

Outside the gaol a considerable crowd had gathered, filling the Crumlin Road and spilling into its side streets. Many were on their way to work and had taken time out to be there at the critical moment. Others hung out of the upstairs windows of the houses opposite the gaol in the hope of catching sight of the condemned man. There was, of course, little for them to see, though by standing on tiptoe at one part of the road it was just possible to see the very top of the scaffold. A few minutes before 8.00 am, the prison bell had begun to toll its dismal message that all was prepared. Then a few minutes past the hour, the black flag was hoisted, signalling that Daly was dead. By the time the body was taken down, at 9.00 am, the crowd had dispersed and all had returned to normal in the outside world. The corpse was lowered into a black-painted plain deal coffin and placed under the scaffold. At 12.30 pm, an inquest jury was gathered in the gaol's boardroom and led down to the gallows to view the body, which "bore no evidence of contortion; the mouth was partially open, and on the neck beneath the chin was a slight mark where the rope had encircled it". The jury found, as in all cases, that the executed man had been lawfully hanged. Shortly after the inquest concluded, Daly's body was stripped of clothing and the coffin filled to the brim with quicklime to aid decomposition. The lid was screwed down and the coffin lowered into an unmarked grave alongside the previous two victims of the gallows.

It had been the Capital Punishment Amendment Act of 1868 that had brought an end to the spectacle of hanging people in front of a howling crowd. The last public execution in Britain was that of Michael Barrett, hanged at Newgate Prison by William Calcraft on 26 May 1868. Barrett had been convicted for his part in an attempt by the Fenians to free Irish prisoners by detonating a bomb outside Clerkenwell House of Detention in London. Twelve people died in the explosion, which demolished part of a wall.

Daly's execution was the fourth in Ulster since the reforms. The others had been at Downpatrick, Cavan and Omagh. The last of these involved the infamous Thomas Hartley Montgomery, a police officer who hacked a Northern Bank cashier to death during a robbery. He underwent three trials before a verdict of guilty was delivered, after which he faked insanity in a last desperate bid to escape the gallows. He was hanged at Omagh Gaol in August 1873.

The infamous Thomas Hartley Montgomery, executed in Omagh Gaol in August 1873, was one of the first men in Ulster to be hanged out of the public gaze. A serving RIC officer, his three trials and ultimate conviction for the murder of a Northern Bank cashier in Newtownstewart – whom he beat to death with a billhook to steal £1,605 – caused a sensation in its day. (News Letter)

Execution of Arthur McKeown

14 January 1889

MURDER IS NOT A crime of the criminal classes but of amateurs, the Royal Commission of 1949-53 concluded. It was fair comment. While a handful of executions carried out at Crumlin Road Gaol followed killings perpetrated during robberies, just one was committed by a truly professional criminal. The rest were, at worst, petty crooks. The majority of those who ended up on the gallows, however, were as the result of domestic circumstances, where the only crime committed was the actual murder itself. Such was the case with the next man to have his neck broken at the end of a rope in the Crumlin Road Gaol.

Arthur McKeown savagely beat to death his common-law wife for refusing to leave her lover to attend a sick child. It was what the newspapers of the day would have termed a "melancholy drama". Described as an "ardent Fenian," McKeown was a man of strong political sentiments. As a teenager he had headed a procession to Hannahstown on 15 August, riding a white horse

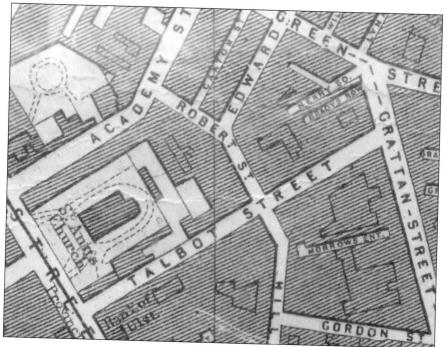

The Ordnance Survey map of 1888 shows Robert Street ran along the back of St Anne's Church, with Morrow's Entry, where McKeown had caught up with his common-law wife, just a short distance away along Hill Street.

and dressed as Robert Emmet – who ironically also ended his days on the scaffold. That parade, like the 1803 Rebellion, ended in chaos when loyalists attacked it. The marchers retreated to Millfield where they were hemmed in for several hours.

McKeown married as a young man, but the relationship failed. In time he took up with Mary Jane Phillips, who bore him two sons. It was not a match made in heaven. She was a drunkard who periodically went off with lovers. He also drank too much and regularly resorted to violence. The couple's neighbours in Belfast's Robert Street, off Academy Street, were continually disturbed by vicious rows, at least one of which resulted in McKeown landing in prison for a time. In July 1888, Mary Jane left him and went to live with another man. McKeown, who described himself as a car driver although he had been without work for a considerable time, took charge of the children for whom he genuinely cared. Nonetheless, having been abandoned obviously angered him and when one of the youngsters fell ill he decided it was time Mary Jane came home.

On 25 August 1888, he went looking for her at the home of Anne McCabe in Morrow's Entry, off Hill Street, arriving shortly before 10.30 pm. He insisted on searching the house, forcing Mrs McCabe to strike a match so he could peer through the darkness of the upstairs bedrooms, but without joy. Infuriated, he turned to the woman and told her, "Well, Mrs McCabe, you have done that neat to get her out of the way, but once I get her I'll put her that she will not run away – I'll put an end to her." In fact, Mary Jane was hiding in the kitchen of the house and chose that moment, when she looked to have got away with it, to rush from the room to meet McKeown with the words, "Arthur, I'm here, I am yours and you are mine." The fine sentiments failed to wash with McKeown, who grabbed her by the throat, forcing her down on to a seat, and demanding she come home. When she refused he struck her the first of five blows with his clenched fist, each drawing blood with the help of a ring he wore. "It is hard to go home to be killed," Mary Jane reportedly told him at one stage. McKeown eventually dragged her out into the street, pulling her along until she conceded and began walking alongside him.

Less than two hours later, at 12.15 am, McKeown was spotted in Robert Street standing opposite his own house by Margaret Crommie, a neighbour who sometimes helped look after the children. She called over to him and he told her Mary Jane was either dead or dying. She, in turn, summoned a police patrol that was by chance passing along the street, and the officers found the woman's body lying on the floor in a pool of blood. According to a police account, an effort had been made to clean up some of the mess. A short

Rough sketches of the house in Robert Street where Mary Jane Phillips was murdered; the bedroom where she met her end; the killer and his victim. *(Belfast Telegraph)*

distance away was a bed on which the youngest of the couple's children, a boy of six, lay sleeping. McKeown, apparently without prompting, then launched into an account of the evening, which was noted down by an officer and read to the court at the Ulster Winter Assizes held in the County Courthouse, Crumlin Road, in December that year:

> "You need not be uneasy about her, she has often been this way before. All the woman wants is to get pumped, then she will be all right. The fact of the matter is she has me robbed. She went away in July last, taking £7 or £8 with her and when she got me away at the Maze races she took two or three more out of that chest of drawers. Tonight I got her in a house in Morrow's Entry, and brought her home. Shortly afterwards we went to bed. I was lying at the wall, and she next the floor. About eleven o'clock the children awakened me, saying their mother was at the drawer again. When I got up she was lying as you see her. I then rose and went out and told Maggie Crommie. She said it would be better to tell the police. There was a bottle of whisky on the drawer when we went to bed, and if you were to see all that's left of it. I suppose she was drunk and fell out of bed. Do you accuse me of giving her foul play?"

The police did, indeed, think he had given her "foul play" and charged him a few hours later. The jury agreed, particularly after hearing the catalogue of injuries uncovered by the doctors who carried out a postmortem on Mary Jane's body two days after the killing. These included eight broken ribs, a ruptured small intestine and severe bruising to the chest and abdomen, swelling around the left eye and cuts about the right, a bruised lower lip, a cut on the chin which went to the bone, a two-inch wound to the jaw, lacerations and bruising to the left cheek, and damage to the nose. A loss of blood caused by the severing of the aorta was cited as being the main cause of death. After only thirty minutes deliberation on the part of the jurors, McKeown was found guilty and sentenced to death. He was lodged in the condemned cell just ten days before Christmas.

Every effort was made to make McKeown, evidently dejected by his situation, as comfortable as possible. A fire was lit in the cell's hearth and the prison medical officer did his bit to warm the inner man by prescribing an ounce of brandy for the prisoner every three hours for the first thirty hours after sentencing. This was reduced to two bottles of stout and three ounces of whiskey every day up until the Lord Lieutenant turned down a plea for mercy, when it was raised to five ounces of whiskey plus the bottles of stout. McKeown was also entitled to half an ounce of tobacco per day. Even so, no

THE ROBERT STREET MURDER.

EXECUTION

OF

ARTHUR M'KEOWN.

THE SCENE ON THE SCAFFOLD.

THE INQUEST.

SKETCH OF THE FELON'S LIFE.

YESTERDAY morning, at the statutory hour of eight o'clock, Arthur M'Keown, convicted of the murder of Mary Jane Phillips in August last, paid the full penalty of his offence on the scaffold. The morning was unusually fine; there was a slight frost in the air, and the accompanying haze or fog delayed the coming daylight. It was not the morning for the dread work that was about to be done inside the walls of the county prison. As early as seven o'clock, just as the lamps were being turned out, the public were astir, and as they wended their way towards the jail gates, there was a manifest feeling of curiosity exhibited on each countenance as to the companionships that were being formed. From Carlisle Circus, up to the grey, dull walls inside of which the unfortunate man was confined, knots of men and women blocked the footpaths, discussing the sensationalism of the hour. They were chiefly of that class in whose favour times never change, and with which the world still wages war. As the minutes rolled past, the crowds increased, and as the sun had now substituted the stars, a glance round the eager throng indicated the quarters from which the majority of them were drawn. Nothing worse, however, marked their conduct than the pleasantries peculiar to waiting, and the forty members of the Royal Irish Constabulary, under District-Inspector M'Ardle, sheltered in the hall of the Courthouse opposite, were not called upon to interfere. Twenty minutes before eight, the uncomfortable-looking members of the local Press presented themselves at the entrance gates to the prison, and after a preliminary process of self-identification, and a subsequent roll-call on the part of the admitting official, they were placed in the charge of the head warder, Mr. Coulter. The first move was to examine the scaf-

executioner indicated that the preliminary stage had been disposed of, and proceeding through a door to the right the felon was for the first time brought within view of the scaffold. The same downcast, dejected, miserable appearance remained, and, as far as could be observed, he never lifted his eyes nor exhibited the least concern while thus walking to his doom. Berry now directed his progress, and, pointing out his position on the drop, it was assumed without apparent emotion. The final act was a short one. The white cap was produced, and placed over his eyes, the legs were strapped, the assistant handed the executioner the noose, which he adjusted with magical dexterity, and stepping aside he touched the lever, and Arthur M'Keown was launched into eternity. Just before the bolt was drawn he prayed in a loud voice, "Lord Jesus receive my soul," "Into Thy hands, O Lord, I commend my spirit," the three last words of which he had barely uttered ere his lips were sealed for ever. There was no "dull thud," as often marks an execution, the opening of the drop and the slight rattling of the rope were the only sounds audible to those at a distance of only three or four yards. Passing down below Dr. Stewart was already there, watch in hand, watching the indications that presented themselves in the features and body of the unfortunate M'Keown. After an interval of half a minute, there were two or three sharp twitches on the left cheek and eye, visible by the uplifting of the white cloth, but beyond this there was no evidence of life. Berry assured all present that death was instantaneous, and that the execution was one of the most successful he had ever conducted. After a few minutes the straps were removed from the legs and arms, and the white cap being pulled aside, showed the face to be somewhat livid, the eyes half closed, and the tongue slightly protruding—in reality, a sickening spectacle. It may be added that the unfortunate man, since the refusal of the prayers of the memorials, has attended with marked devotion to the ministrations of the prison chaplain, and was quite resigned to his fate. He did not retire to rest till two o'clock yesterday morning, and after having a broken sleep for three hours, he arose at five o'clock. The chaplain was again in attendance at six, and celebrated mass and the holy communion. The culprit, when asked, refused to partake of any breakfast, and he died without making any formal confession of his guilt. The black flag was hoisted just on the stroke of eight o'clock, and the large crowds having their morbid curiosity satisfied, quietly dispersed. With reference to our "stop-press" edition issued yesterday morning, we may state that the *Belfast News-Letter* containing the full facts of the execution, as witnessed by our special representative, was on sale on the streets of the city at twenty minutes to nine o'clock. This was the only account by an eye-witness, and written actually *after* the occurrence, which was available until considerably after that hour. It is but fair to add that the prison arrangements were all that could be desired. The Press are under deep obligations to the Under-Sheriff for his extreme courtesy, and also to Mr. M'Kenna, the deputy-governor of the jail, for the interest he took in giving them all the facilities at his disposal for the performance of what to them was anything but a pleasing duty.

THE INQUEST.

At nine o'clock the body was cut down, and at a quarter-past twelve o'clock the Coroner (Dr. Dill) held an inquest on the remains in the Boardroom of the County Jail.

Mr. Hugh M'Neile M'Cormick, Clerk of the Crown; Mr. Henry Haigh Bottomley, Sub-Sheriff for the County of Antrim; Mr. Jeremiah M'Kenna, Deputy-Governor of the jail; and District-Inspector M'Ardle were in attendance.

The following gentlemen were sworn upon the jury:—Messrs. John Trainor, publican, Old Lodge Road; Thomas Conroy, civil bill officer, 13, Ponsonby Avenue; Robert Dick, pensioner, Woodland Avenue; Robert Wilson, T.C., contractor, 8 Cavendish Terrace; Henry Scott, druggist, Ria Street; Patrick Quigley, spirit merchant, 18, Hillman Street; Adam Turner, auctioneer, Clifton Street; William Moore, traveller, Lincoln Avenue; Patrick Leonard, hotelkeeper, Duncairn Arms; John Corkorin, R.I.C., pensioner; John M'Auley, lamplighter, 4, Ashton Street;

M'Keown was tried, convicted, and sentenced to be hanged on January 14th. This morning, at eight o'clock, I saw that warrant carried out. In pursuance of the warrant I attended at the County Antrim Jail, and formally demanded the body of Arthur M'Keown from the Deputy-Governor. This having been done, I handed the condemned man over to James Berry, public executioner, who carried out the sentence in my presence. That sentence was that he should be hanged by the neck until he was dead. I waited until the doctor stated that he was dead, and in about an hour after I saw the body cut down. I was in court during the trial. I heard the verdict of guilty returned by a jury of the County of Antrim, and heard the sentence of death pronounced by the Right Honourable Mr. Justice Holmes.

Mr. ROBERT WILSON—I suppose you don't know where Berry is now?

Witness—I do not.

Mr. WILSON—When did you last see him?

Witness—I think it was about a quarter-past nine o'clock. He asked me if he could go away, and I said he could, as I did not want him any longer.

Mr. LEONARD—Do the implements with which the execution was carried out belong to him?

Witness—Yes, the rope and pinioning straps are his.

Mr. WILSON—Was it a rope or a chain that went round the man's neck?

Witness—It was a rope, of course.

Mr. LEONARD—Don't you think it would be more satisfactory for the jurors if they could have an opportunity of seeing the rope or other appliances with which death was caused?

Witness—I don't see that it would.

Mr. LEONARD—I think that in a case of this kind we should have the evidence of the executioner, and should also see the rope with which a man's life is taken away. I think it would be more satisfactory.

Witness—I do not agree with you at all, but, of course, I shall not discuss the matter.

Mr. RANKIN—I think that the proper thing would be that the executioner should be detained until after the inquest for the purpose of giving evidence as to how the sentence was carried out. He alone can give that evidence.

Mr. LEONARD—It is necessary that we should have his evidence.

Witness—The coroner will direct you as to whether the evidence is sufficient or not, but, in my opinion, no good object could be secured by the production of the executioner.

CORONER—Gentlemen, we will have the medical evidence, and that must be your guide in finding out the cause of death. Neither of the gentlemen that we have had produced, not even the executioner if he were here, could give you authoritative evidence as to the cause of death. That evidence must come from the doctor, and we will have it now. Of course, what the juror has just said is perfectly right, as an expression of opinion, as any juror has a right to express his opinion upon this or any other matter connected with the inquiry, but I must tell you that the only authority in law for the cause of death is the medical testimony, which we will hear in a moment or two.

Witness—I may tell you that Berry stated that, although he has carried out many executions, he has never yet been required to attend and give evidence before a jury.

CORONER—There is no statute law upon the subject, but precedent and custom have fixed it, and never within my memory had the public executioner been present or given evidence before a jury. That is the custom.

Mr. LEONARD—But it is not too late to change that custom, and in the opinion of myself and others of the jury the executioner should be present to give evidence.

Mr. SHIELDS—As a juror, and I would ask the representatives of the Press to take a note of it, I protest against this practice of smuggling the hangman out by the back door after an execution.

Witness—I think such a statement is unwarrantable, and should not be made.

CORONER—Now, gentlemen, under the law, as it stands at present, these executions are carried out in private, and, I think, most properly so, in the interests of public decency; but although the execution is private, this inquiry is quite public, and with that view, I left instructions that no person having any interest whatever in the inquiry should be excluded from it.

Mr. WILSON—Consequently, we should have all the evidence before us.

CORONER—You will have all that is necessary or available. We will now take the evidence of the medical officer of the jail.

John Stewart stated—I am medical officer of her Majesty's Prison of Belfast, and I was present at

How the *News Letter,* which put out a special edition on the morning of McKeown's execution, reported the Robert Street murderer's demise.

amount of drink could drown out the knowledge of his impending doom. His last night, apart from about three hours tossing and turning in bed, was spent pacing the floor. At 5.00 am he gave up all thought of sleep and prepared instead to meet his God, celebrating Mass with a priest an hour later. He refused breakfast, and turned down the opportunity to confess his guilt. A few moments after 8.00 am, on 14 January 1889, the solemn procession consisting of the Under Sheriff of County Antrim, the deputy Governor, the prison doctor, two clergymen, McKeown and several warders, arrived at the scaffold. As they passed along the passageway the prisoner could be heard joining in the responses to the prayers for the dying being recited by the priest, whose voice faltered at times as he struggled to restrain his own emotions. Within three or four yards of the end of the corridor, executioner James Berry stepped forward and pinioned McKeown's arms.

A *News Letter* reporter, whose account appeared in a special edition of the newspaper published within three-quarters of an hour of the trap doors falling, takes up the story:

> "A sign from the executioner indicated that the preliminary stage had been disposed of, and proceeding through a door to the right the felon was for the first time brought within view of the scaffold. The same downcast, dejected, miserable appearance remained, and, as far as could be observed, he never lifted his eyes nor exhibited the least concern while thus walking to his doom. Berry now directed his progress, and pointing out his position on the drop, it was assumed without apparent emotion. The final act was a short one. The white cap was produced, and placed over his eyes, the legs were strapped, the assistant handed the executioner the noose, which he adjusted with magical dexterity, and stepping aside he touched the lever, and Arthur McKeown was launched into eternity. Just before the bolt was drawn he prayed in a loud voice, 'Lord Jesus receive my soul, into Thy Hands, O Lord, I commend my spirit,' the three last words of which he had barely uttered ere his lips were sealed for ever. There was no 'dull thud' as often marks an execution, the opening of the drop and the slight rattling of the rope were the only sounds audible to those at a distance of only three or four yards."

Within seconds the prison doctor, watch in hand, was examining the body for signs of life. The heart was still beating and McKeown's left cheek and eye twitched several times, but nonetheless life was declared to be extinct. A few minutes later the straps binding the arms and feet were removed and the white cap pulled aside to show the face to be "somewhat livid, the eyes half closed, and the tongue slightly protruding – in reality, a sickening spectacle".

An inquest opened in the prison boardroom at 12.15 pm, with the jurors, once sworn in, being conducted by the deputy Governor to the end of the passage where McKeown's body lay in the traditional plain wood coffin. A warder removed the lid and each member of the jury viewed the corpse in turn. They returned to the boardroom in a hostile mood and demanded to know why Berry had not remained in the prison to be quizzed about the execution. They then asked to see the rope used, but were again to be disappointed, as the hangman had taken it with him. Finally they complained about a swelling around McKeown's eye, which had been clearly visible at the viewing. At long last, however, it was agreed that the execution had been a lawful killing and McKeown took his place in an unmarked grave to the rear of the prison.

* * *

Execution of John Gilmour

17 August 1894

AS LYLE GARDNER STOOD in front of his kitchen fire undressing for bed, on 30 April 1894, he must have wondered just what had happened to his snug existence of barely a week before. His only daughter, Jane, had given birth to an illegitimate child eight days previously and now relationships between himself and the Gilmour family next door were strained after the girl had claimed their son, John, was the baby's father. Indeed, less than half-an-hour earlier that evening Gardner and his wife had had an argument with the young man on their own doorstep, with the allegations flying thick and fast. The incident was still troubling the old man as he prepared to retire for the night. The rest of the household, consisting of his daughter and new grandchild, Gardner's infant son William, and servant boy John Rodgers were already in bed. Only he and his wife, who was busy raking out the ashes from the fire, remained downstairs as the kitchen clock ticked towards 9.00 pm.

Suddenly a shot rang out, the retort coming from a gun discharged through a window, and Gardner fell wounded. His wife managed to catch hold of him, saving the old man from crashing to the floor. She screamed for help and managed to raise Jane, who helped her pull Gardner on to the bed. Dr Peter Camac was sent for, and he in turn called for the assistance of Dr Robert Craig, but Gardner lost his battle for life before the second medic arrived, and less than an hour after being shot. A postmortem showed he had suffered more than forty pellet wounds, mostly to the abdomen.

A man of 78, and twice married, Gardner had been an active member of his community. He had spent what turned out to be his last day working a pair of horses on his smallholding at Ballyhivistock, a few miles outside the village of Dervock, in north Antrim. The Gilmours' farmhouse stood just across the way, little more than 600 yards separating the front doors. Relationships between the families, up until the birth of the child on 22 April, had been extremely good. However, the possibility of a lawsuit to establish 21-year-old John Gilmour as the father of Jane's child, and so force him to pay maintenance, had understandably cast a shadow over the friendship. Under the law, Jane herself could not take any action against Gilmour, but Gardner, as her father, could instigate court proceedings for the wrong done to his daughter. That, it was later argued, was the sole motive for the farmer's murder.

The birth of the child had come as a complete shock to Gardner and his wife for Jane, by starving herself to compensate for her developing bulge, had managed to conceal her pregnancy from them right up until she went into labour. Jane, on the other hand, had told Gilmour some six months previously that she was expecting his child, but he had turned his back on her. But once the baby was born, and the allegation made that he had fathered it, Gilmour could no longer simply turn a blind eye. Instead he cooked up a clumsy, poorly thought through plan to kill the old man and so, he thought, save the embarrassment and shame of a court case. On the afternoon of the murder, about 3.00 pm, Gilmour set off with a horse to Dervock, less than three miles away, and left it at the village blacksmith's to be shod. He then travelled on to Ballymoney in a cart hired from McCann's and driven by one of their employees, David McBride. The two separated on arrival, with Gilmour heading for Hamill's shop, which stocked a wide range of goods. There he bought a "cheap fowling piece" for £2, some powder and shot, as well as other odds and ends. Gilmour, who made the unusual request to have the gun wrapped in brown paper, returned to the shop later to collect the weapon just before heading back to Dervock. He called for the horse and returned home at 7.45 pm, feeding the animal before having supper himself. None of the family remembered him bringing the gun he had bought a few hours earlier into the house. About 8.30 pm, the Gardners, with the exception of Jane, were sitting in their kitchen when suddenly Mrs Gardner let out a scream after spotting a face peering in the window at them. She and the old farmer rushed out the front door to see who was there. The servant boy Rodgers, meanwhile,

Lyle Gardner's remains lie in a churchyard at Derrykeighan, a couple of miles outside Dervock. The headstone, erected in 1932 to his son's memory, makes no mention of the circumstances of the father's death. *(Author)*

had the sense to go to the window, where he saw Gilmour heading off across the fields. Possibly realising he had been spotted, Gilmour changed direction and instead confronted the Gardners at the front of the house. "Are you going to lay the blame of this wean on me?" he demanded to know. They were not accusing him, the Gardners told Gilmour, but their daughter had named him as the father. Gilmour hit back with an accusation of his own. "I will teach you there are many more fathers than one of that child," he said. He demanded to know if the old man intended taking him to court over the claims, but couldn't get a satisfactory answer. After a further exchange of words, the conversation was broken off and Gilmour apparently headed off. Approximately twenty minutes later the fatal shot was fired through the same window Gilmour had been spotted at earlier.

Within minutes of the shooting, in an apparent bid to establish an alibi,

Gilmour was at the door of Samuel Wilson, a labourer who worked for his father. He stayed there for close on two hours before returning home. The police, meanwhile, had been summoned to the Gardners, with Sergeant John Slattery and two constables arriving at the scene shortly before midnight. It didn't take them long to identify a chief suspect, and they were soon crossing the short distance to the Gilmour's farm, where they found the young man in bed. A search of his coat quickly turned up the powder and shot bought earlier. His biggest mistake, however, was volunteering the information that he had been at Samuel Wilson's at 9.00 pm – for no one had mentioned when Lyle Gardiner had been shot. Gilmour was promptly arrested and imprisoned in Crumlin Road Gaol. The murder weapon was found a few days later, hidden in gorse bushes within 300 yards of the Gardners' house.

Gilmour appeared before Mr Justice Gibson at the County Antrim Assizes in July 1894. As was normal in murder trials, the court was crowded long before the defendant appeared, with people thronging the doorways. Throughout the two-day hearing Gilmour sat forward in the dock, apparently paying great attention to the proceedings, though not displaying any obvious understanding of his predicament. The jury retired at 1.15 pm on Thursday, 19 July, returning at 2.45 pm with a verdict of guilty, but with a strong recommendation of mercy because of his youth and previous good character. As the judge donned the black cap and delivered his sentence of death, Gilmour alone in the packed courtroom appeared unaffected by the solemnity of the moment.

The day of execution was set for Friday, 18 August 1894. For the first time in the history of hangings in Belfast, the Press was excluded. The decision by the prison authorities was consistent with a policy being adopted by Governors across the British Isles, prompted by the Home Office, and was aimed at putting a stop to newspaper reports of botched executions. Gilmour, who was guarded by two warders throughout his imprisonment, is said to have slept fairly well on his last night. At 5.00 am, when the Governor visited the condemned cell, he was already up and dressed. An hour later the two Presbyterian clergy who had attended him throughout, the Rev Dr Crawford and the Rev Joseph Northey, arrived at the prison and remained with Gilmour to the end.

He breakfasted "very sparingly" on tea and toast and thanked everyone for their care and kindness during his last days. Gilmour is said to have confessed his guilt and to have shaken hands with the Governor, the warders who had made up his guard day and night, and the two clergymen. The usual solemn procession was then formed, with Dr Crawford offering up the prayers from

The view along one of the gaol's wings, taken shortly after the prison closed to inmates. *(Irish News)*

the front and Gilmour, flanked by two warders and walking "with a firm step", joining in. As they approached the scaffold, Scott, the executioner, stepped out from one of the cells and quickly pinioned his arms. The party then passed through a doorway on to the scaffold platform. As the hangman completed his preparations, Gilmour prayed, "Lord, have mercy on my soul; into Thy hands I commend my spirit." As the bolt was drawn, he is said to have called out, "Farewell to all till we meet again." The scaffold, as for McKeown, had been erected at the end of the prison's D wing, close to the Mater Hospital, with the condemned cell some thirty feet away.

The hoisting of the black flag immediately afterwards, and the ringing of the prison bell either side of the execution, let the large crowd gathered outside on the Crumlin Road know that Gilmour had paid the ultimate price for his crime. All but a handful of the people had disappeared by the time the 10.00 am inquest was convened. The jurors, before being sworn in, were taken to the condemned cell to see the body, which had hung for an hour before being taken down and placed in a coffin. They were also shown the gallows and had its workings explained to them by a warder. Back in the boardroom, the prison doctor, Dr Stewart, assured them that death had been "almost instantaneous". He refused to be drawn on an exact time but estimated it had taken Gilmour less than three minutes to die. City Coroner ES Finnigan, in an unusual step for a man in his position, went on the record to oppose capital punishment. Pointing out that in previous years hangings in public had been a "disgrace to their common humanity," he said he felt sure that some, if not all the jurors, probably wished they had been banned altogether rather than merely performed out of sight. The jurors ruled that the death was legal; they also decided to send letters of sympathy to both the Gilmour and Gardner families.

CHAPTER NINE

New century, old habits

Oh, it is not as bad as a bad marriage.

Condemned man William Woods

Execution of William Woods

11 January 1901

THE MOST REMARKABLE THING about the hanging of William Woods on Friday, 11 January 1901, was that it had not taken place a decade earlier. With perhaps one other unproven exception, the 58-year-old tramp was the only man executed at Crumlin Road Gaol who had killed before the murder that finally booked his appointment with the executioner.

Woods' lucky escape was some eleven years before his death. Described as a dealer, in reality he and common-law wife Mary Irwin were down-and-outs who travelled around County Londonderry gathering rags and reselling them to finance their alcoholism. The pair, both of whom were separated from their respective spouses, had been together for some nine years by 1890. On 5 July that year, a Saturday, they were arrested within an hour of each other for drunkenness in the village of Claudy, and taken to the local barracks to sleep it off. After some six hours in the police cells, they were released together shortly before midnight, and were last seen wandering off towards Londonderry. As events were to show, they found shelter that night in a shed at Gortnaran, about a mile from Claudy. At 3.15 am a farmer, Samuel Crooks, was awakened by what he thought was a scream. He got out of bed and peered from his window into the darkness, but could see nothing unusual and so returned to his slumbers. A few hours later, and with his working day well under way, Crooks went to collect his cart from the shed. There a sight so horrific it would have turned the strongest of stomachs confronted him. Mary Irwin, her throat cut, lay in a pool of blood on the floor. Her head, held against a cartwheel by a rope tied in a noose around her neck, stared straight ahead, while the torso lay on one shoulder. A scythe, found on the other side of the cart, was still dripping with her blood.

The next day, in what must have been a harrowing ordeal, Mary's 19-year-old daughter, Matilda Irwin, was brought to the shed from her home in Fountain Street, Londonderry, to identify her mother's body – which had been left as it had been found, still tied to the cart. She also attended an inquest, held in Crooks' farmhouse, where jurors were told the fatal wound had partially separated two vertebrae, finishing perhaps an inch short of decapitation. Meanwhile, thirty RIC officers in plain clothes scarred the countryside for Woods, who had not been seen since leaving Claudy barracks. After spending two days hiding in a haystack, he was eventually captured by Head Constable Webster after hunger forced him out into the open. When arrested he was still wearing the heavily bloodstained clothes he had been dressed in when he cut Mary's throat.

Justice, no matter what else could be said about it, was swift. On 8 July, within hours of being captured, Woods was brought before a magistrate in Claudy to see if he had a case to answer. It was a short sitting. Woods, in what proved to be a typical gesture, brought matters

Woods was fortunate to escape with his life after being convicted of cutting the throat of his common-law wife with a scythe. His luck ran out, however, when he committed a chillingly similar killing a decade later. (News Letter)

THE COUNTY DERRY MURDER.

WOODS PLEADS GUILTY.

SPECIAL TELEGRAM.

DERRY, TUESDAY.—To-day a magisterial investigation into the brutal murder of a woman, which took place a few miles from Londonderry on Sunday last was held. The Court sat in Claudy, and the prisoner, who was arrested yesterday, after hiding without food in a plantation for two days, was put forward, and charged with the wilful murder of Mary Woods, *alias* Irwin. Evidence was given that the prisoner and the murdered woman, though both married to other living individuals, had cohabited for nine or ten years. A daughter of the deceased, after severe cross-examination, admitted having heard the prisoner several times threaten to have her mother's life. In reply to a question why she refused to answer at first, the girl said she did not want to be too hard on the murderer. Other evidence as to frequent quarrels between the two was then given. It was also proved that the man and woman were seen approaching the place where the dead body of the latter was afterwards found, and the prisoner's clothes, all blood-stained, were produced. Crooks, the farmer in whose outhouse the woman was found, was being examined, when the prisoner interposed, and said—There is no use keeping you any more. It was I did it. I killed the woman, and that is all there is about it. There need not be any more talk. The prisoner was cautioned, but repeated his statement. Medical evidence was then given, and the inquiry was adjourned till Monday next. The prisoner was removed to Derry Jail.

to a speedy conclusion when he interrupted farmer Crooks' evidence to tell the court, "There is no use keeping you any more. It was I did it. I killed the woman, and that is all there is about it. There need not be any more talk." On 22 July the scene switched to the Crown Court and the Londonderry Assizes. The evidence was damning and it took the jury just fifteen minutes to come back with a verdict of guilty – but of manslaughter, not murder. Mr Justice Johnson, in sentencing him to twelve years in gaol, told Woods he had that day "stood face-to-face with death," and his escape had been a narrow one. Woods was no stranger to gaol, and had more than thirty convictions to his name. He also bragged to officers, while in Claudy barracks the night before the murder, that he had been thrown into police cells some 159 times – not necessarily an accurate figure, but a clear indication of the type of life he led.

With remission, Woods was released from gaol in July 1899 and quickly returned to his old ways, but this time his hunting ground was County Antrim. Instead of rags, he now peddled in needles and pins. He often tramped the roads of the Bushmills area and it was there he became friendly with a widow, Bridget McGivern, with whom he often called and occasionally stayed. On the afternoon of 25 September 1900, Woods bought a razor at Taggart's shop in Bushmills, paying one shilling and sixpence for it. It was, apparently, an investment for he told the assistant who served him that he

intended selling it on to a customer in the country. He then headed out to the McGivern cabin at Eagry, on the fringes of the town, where he waited with the widow's children, both boys, aged fourteen and three, until their mother's arrival about 6.30 pm. Woods joined the family for tea and then settled down in front of the fire with a bottle of whiskey, pouring the widow a glass and drinking the rest himself. When that was done, he pulled a further half-pint bottle

William Woods, a double killer, was quite a character. He put on weight while in prison awaiting execution and only appears to have realised the seriousness of his situation in his final days. *(Belfast Telegraph)*

from inside his coat and, again pouring a tot for Mrs McGivern, consumed the remainder. Woods was evidently in good form, giving the elder boy, Charles, a penny as reward for going for water and later sixpence to go to see a menagerie coming to Bushmills. Eventually it was time to retire, the woman sleeping with the two children in one bed and Woods, pulling off his coat and boots, lying on top of the only other bed. Shortly before 6.00 am the next morning, the oldest boy awoke to discover his mother was no longer lying with him and his brother. Squinting in the cold dawn light, he could just make out a figure lying on the other bed. Realising it was his mother, he went over and tried to rouse her and found her flesh warm to the touch, but she would never waken again for her throat had been cut. Grabbing the younger child he rushed from the house and across to a neighbour, Matilda Curry, banging on her door and shouting, "For God's sake let me and the child in, for Willie Woods has cut the head of me ma." Mrs Curry set out to Bushmills to alert the police, but met a party of officers already on their way. About the same time the boy had found his mother's body, Woods had arrived at the barracks. Smelling of alcohol and covered in blood, he told the sergeant, "The woman in Eagry is dead. I killed the woman, and that is all there is about it. We were both drunk. There is the blood." The police found Mrs McGivern's body lying partially on its left side and her throat cut "ear to ear". She was almost naked, apart for a strip of a nightdress across her shoulders and covering one breast. Blood was everywhere but concentrated on the chest, face and neck. Oddly, two half crowns lay in the blood on the bed. Woods' muffler had been thrown across her throat and his coat propped up her head. A postmortem examination showed the throat wound to be eight inches long. As before, it had penetrated right to the vertebral column, just short of completely removing the head. There was also a wound on the left arm about three inches in length.

One can only speculate as to what happened that morning. The fire in the house, raked out the previous evening, had been re-lit, presumably by Mrs McGivern. Perhaps she disturbed Woods while about this task and he attacked her, possibly with rape in mind judging by the state of the woman's nightclothes. That, however, would suggest a struggle and there was no evidence of that, with neither the children nor the neighbours hearing anything. Perhaps the sleeping Woods had been reliving the nightmare of the previous killing, and it had turned into a re-enactment on this poor woman. Or perhaps he was genuinely temporarily insane, as his defence was to argue later in court, and didn't know what he was doing. Interestingly, he washed his hands in a bucket of cold water after the killing. He also disposed of the razor

X McGIVERNS HOUSE
DOOR GUARDED BY POLICEMAN

THE CORONER
(DR WOODSIDE)

JOHN M'GIVERN
AGED 2½ YRS

CHAS M'GIVERN
AGED 14 YRS

BAIRD. BELFAST

POLICE BARRACK AT BUSHMILLS

SERGEANT WALKER.

The *Belfast Telegraph* featured these sketches from the inquest into the death. Sergeant Walker gave evidence at the initial hearing into Bridget McGivern's death and Dr Woodside, the coroner, heard how she had suffered a series of injuries as well as having her throat cut. *(Belfast Telegraph)* in a derelict building close to the police station where he gave himself up. It was found on 17 November 1900, by children and handed over to the RIC.

On 12 December 1900, William Woods stood trial in front of Mr Justice Madden at the Ulster Winter Assizes. The jury took half-an-hour to find him guilty of murder and his execution date was set for 11 January 1901. As he left the dock, Woods uttered the immortal line, "Oh, it is not as bad as a bad marriage." This apparent indifference continued throughout his first three weeks in the condemned cell, with Woods joking with his warders as to the quality of whiskey he would receive in gaol. He also ate heartily, putting on 20 lbs between his conviction and death.

As the day of execution grew closer, however, and any hopes of a reprieve faded, Woods grew depressed, refusing to eat altogether in his last few days. He also began taking a greater interest in the spiritual offerings of the Church of Ireland chaplain, the Rev Dr Spence, who, as custom demanded, spent the last few hours with the condemned man. At 8.00 am, executioner Scott entered the cell and pinioned Woods' arms. He was led, with the help of two warders, the few yards onto the gallows. With no assistant, the hangman completed the process on his own, securing the legs, placing the white hood over the head and adjusting the rope about the neck. As Scott stood back to push the lever, Woods muttered a few lines of prayer before he was launched into eternity. At 5 ft 5 ins and weighing 133 lbs on the day of execution, he was given a drop of some 7 ft 10 ins.

The tolling of the prison bell and the hoisting of the black flag told the crowd outside the prison walls, made up mainly of the 'lower classes', that the execution had been carried out. After hanging for the usual hour, the body was taken down and placed in a black-painted coffin lined with wood shavings. Woods was dressed in a rough brown jacket, dark trousers and black socks. Shortly after 11.00 am, the inquest jury viewed the corpse. Journalists were also admitted at this point and one recorded:

"The deceased was fully dressed in his own clothes, excepting his boots, hat and collar, and it was quite evident that when the neck was dislocated a quantity of blood issued from his nose. His face was slightly bulged, and his left eye partially open. It was difficult to see the mark of the rope on the neck in consequence of his beard – indeed, there was little to make one believe that he had not died a natural death."

Dr John Stewart, the prison doctor, agreed it had been a textbook hanging, "It appeared to be most skilful. I am prepared to say death was instantaneous. There was not a quiver of a muscle of the body."

Execution of Richard Justin

19 August 1909

Bridget McWilliams was the salt of the earth. While most other people were prepared to turn their backs on an unmarried mother, she went out of her way to help. Every morning for four years she took on the role of unpaid nanny to Annie Thompson, taking the girl into her own home to allow her mother, Jane, to continue working. Even after the belated marriage of the child's parents, Mrs McWilliams continued to look after little Annie on a daily basis. She began to become alarmed, however, after noticing bruising on the body of the four-year-old. There were other injuries, too, including a swollen chin, a black eye and a tooth apparently knocked out. But, in February 1909, just as her concerns began to grow into a genuine fear for the child's safety, Annie was stopped coming to Mrs McWilliams' house, staying at home in Lepper Street, in the New Lodge area of Belfast, instead. Annie shared the house with her father, Richard Justin, her mother Jane, and two half-brothers. The first Mrs Justin had died some eight years earlier, before the relationship began which produced Annie out of wedlock.

On 12 March 1909, Jane Justin left the house at 6.00 am as normal to go to work in Whitehouse Mill, to be followed five minutes later by her husband. He, like so many others, was finding it difficult to get a regular job but had been given a place working on the Belfast Corporation relief works for the unemployed in Alexandra Park. Richard returned home at 9.00 am, apparently for breakfast. But within minutes of his arrival he was at the door of Annie Loughlands, who lived in an upstairs room of the same house. His daughter, he told her, had fallen out of bed and was in urgent need of help. While the neighbour stayed with Annie, Richard went off in search of a doctor. It was to no avail. The child, who was unconscious throughout, died at 10.50 am. She was three months short of her fifth birthday.

Within hours of the death the rumours began to fly around. Some told of screams and cries coming from the house; others of the marks seen on the child's body; and all pointed the finger at the father. A postmortem, carried out the next day, seemed to confirm the stories, for the doctors found a litany of injuries. These included some thirty bruises to the chest, arms, thighs and head, though most were several days old. Professor Symmers, who conducted the medical investigation, even went as far as to say they were the worst injuries to a child he had ever seen. Following his evidence at the inquest on 15 March, Richard Justin was arrested and charged with the murder of his daughter.

The case came to trial at the City of Belfast Assizes on 22 July 1909. The

Alexandra Park was opened in 1887 on a 10-acre site. A further 10 acres were purchased in 1908 and a team of workmen, including Richard Justin, laboured to reshape it as part of a relief works scheme. It was from Alexandra Park that Justin returned to his New Lodge home the morning little Annie was found barely alive. *(Courtesy of the National Library of Ireland)*

prosecution, alleging that Annie's demise was the accumulation of months of abuse with the intention of causing her death, produced a series of witnesses to back the assertion. One neighbour told the court she had heard Annie's mother, Jane Justin, cry out on one occasion, "Hit me, and let the child alone," while another, Margaret Craig, who claimed Richard regularly beat the girl when left alone with her, said she had heard Annie cry out, "Da, da, don't beat me anymore." A work colleague of Mrs Justin's, Annie McGeough, was called to repeat Jane's reaction to being told by Justin that Annie had been hurt, "I knew you would finish her at last." Several 'weapons' found in the Justin household, including a piece of wood and an iron rod, were also produced, with allegations made that they were used to beat the child, though there was no evidence to support the claim.

The defence rested on the testimony of Justin's eldest son, also called Richard. He said the three children – himself, his younger brother Jack and Annie – had been lying in the one bed, with the little girl nearest the wall. Shortly before 7.00 am, Annie had awakened and began climbing over the boys to get out of bed. She had trampled on the edge of her nightdress, however, and fell over the side. Her head, he said in evidence, had struck the metal strut of their parents' bed, which was only separated from the children's bed by about eighteen inches. The girl had let out a moan and then lay still on the floor.

BELFAST MORNING NEWS, FRIDAY, AUGUST 20, 1909.

THE EXTREME PENALTY.

Richard Justin Executed in Belfast Jail.

PRISONER'S PENITENCE.

CONDEMNED MAN THANKS COUNSEL FOR ABLE DEFENCE.

The wretched man, Richard Justin, who was condemned to death for the wilful murder of his child at the recent Summer Assizes, suffered the extreme penalty of the law at Belfast Jail yesterday morning. Since his condemnation Justin exhibited great penitence, and was most attentive to the ministrations of his clergyman, the Rev. Mr. Woolley, Unitarian minister. Shortly before eight o'clock Mr. Thomas Stringer, Governor of the Prison, formally handed Justin over to the custody of the High Sheriff (Councillor F. Curley, J.P.) and the Sub-Sheriff (Mr. James Quail). Pierpont, the executioner, then took charge of the prisoner, and commenced his gruesome task. It was but a short distance from the cell to the execution room. Justin, it is said, displayed remarkable fortitude; and so expeditiously did the executioner carry out his

DREADFUL PRELIMINARIES

that in an almost incredibly short space of time the bolt was drawn, and the wretched man launched into eternity. After hanging for some time the body was cut down, and placed in a rough deal shell, in which it was subsequently viewed by the jury previous to the inquest. Outside the jail people, prompted by morbid curiosity, commenced to assemble from an early hour, and from seven o'clock onward the crowd was every moment augmented, many being evidently under the impression that they would witness the hoisting of the sinister black flag. As this custom was abolished some years ago the first intimation to the waiting crowd that

THE GRIM LEGAL TRAGEDY

was complete was the tolling of the prison bell. A little time afterwards the notices required by law were posted on the main gate of the prison buildings. Of these notices there were three. The first announced that the execution would take place at the hour specified, and was posted the previous night. Another, signed by the High Sheriff, Sub-Sheriff, the Governor of the jail, and the clergyman in attendance on the condemned man, declared that the "judgment of death" had been carried out. The third and final notice was a certificate from Dr. Stewart, medical officer of the prison, announcing that "the said Richard Justin was dead."

So far as can be ascertained, Justin met his death with great penitence and fortitude. His farewell to his aged and sorrow-stricken father and mother was piteously painful, and the prison officials whose duty compelled them to be present at the final leave-taking between the condemned man and his relatives were much affected by the scenes of grim and sorrowing grief. One of the

LAST ACTS OF THE CONDEMNED MAN

was to send to his surviving children a number of books which had been presented to him by friends since his sentence. He expressed unbounded gratitude to Mr. Thomas J. Campbell, B.L., who ably and eloquently defended him at his trial, and desired that a sincere message of thanks should be conveyed to that gentleman. Justin atoned for a shocking crime with his life, and in the days that were left him since his condemnation, he undoubtedly expressed deep penitence for the offence that rendered forfeit his existence, and showed his gratitude for the acts of kindness and consideration extended him by the prison officials.

Justin's Crime—Counsel's Eloquent Appeal.

The history of the crime for which Justin paid the extreme penalty is too fresh in the minds of our readers to need recapitulation. In view of his penitence and his expressions of deep gratitude to Mr. Campbell, B.L., for his able defence, it may not be out of place to give the following extracts from counsel's able and eloquent appeal to the jury:—

The Crown, said Mr. Campbell, asked them to say that the prisoner's hands were crimson with the blood of his infant daughter—a crime most foul, cruel, and unnatural, which would cry aloud from earth to Heaven for vengeance. Let them pause and think long and well of what the learned Attorney-General asked them to do—to find him guilty of the destruction, the deliberate destruction of his own child—blood of his blood, bone of his bone—and for no reason. Theirs was the awful duty of sitting in judgment upon life and death. The slow, sure passage of the clock that summer day might have reminded some among them that we are all passing on to the last Assize of all—to the Judgment Throne of the great King of Kings, in Whose sight a thousand years are as yesterday which is past and as a watch in the night. In the eternal tables of His law the Divine Judge has decreed that human life was sacred beyond all gold and silver and precious stones. Little Annie Thompson had passed before that Judgment Throne, and death would be no more for her, nor mourning nor sorrow any more. Could they in their consciences

VISIT HER DEATH ON HER OWN FATHER?

The law for the protection of the good and the repression of the wicked would adjudge that a crime of that crimson dye, upon one so young, so helpless, so tender, deserved the last dread penalty—that blood should atone for blood, and life should pay for life. Their verdict of "Guilty" would mean for the prisoner that, after three or four weeks of agony in the gloom of his condemned cell, a death of shame would await him, and his eyes would never again open to the sun and sky. He (counsel) spoke, therefore, as one who felt he was standing between this man and the scaffold. With all earnestness he begged and implored them to raise their minds high and clear above prejudice. He feared the prejudice which sprung up irresistibly in favour of a weak child alleged to have been

DONE TO DEATH BY A STRONG MAN.

Let the jury pay no regard to anything but the voice of their own consciences and sense of their duty to God and man. In the dreadful straits in which the prisoner now stood he was not deserted by his family. His father, broken with years—who, he (counsel) prayed, would not be broken hereafter with shame—had told them on his oath that the prisoner was a maligned man, and far from being a cruel man, was kind to the dead child. They had heard that bright little fellow, Richard, to whom the man in the dock was never a cruel father. Prisoner's wife was in that court, and of all living beings she could speak best on this awful charge, but the law sealed her mouth. She must sit in silence. She could not go into the witness-box to tell the jury what she knew of it all. What a hard fate was hers! Upon the evidence before them the jury could not, they ought not to, they dared not find the prisoner guilty. They would vindicate their character and honour as

FEARLESS GUARDIANS OF JUSTICE

—justice perpetual and immortal. The Crown asked for that verdict of guilty that would, within a month, by the hand of man, take from the prisoner the life which had been lent him, and which God would ask for again in His own good time, when

(continued)

walls of the said prison, on the 19th day of August, 1909, not more than twenty-fours before the holding of this inquest, and that the body on which this inquest was held is the identical body of the said Richard Justin, adjudged to death as aforesaid."

Subsequent to the inquest the remains were interred within the precincts of the jail.

How the *Belfast Morning News* reported Justin's execution. *(Irish News)*

Richard, picking her up, gently set her back in the bed, being careful not to waken his brother. It was there that his father had found her some two hours later, he told a hushed court. Richard Junior also denied his father beat the girl, but instead accused his stepmother's sister, also named Annie Thompson, of banging the girl's head against a wall several days before the youngster's death. Prof Symmers, who again presented his evidence, admitted a fall as described by Richard could have resulted in the brain haemorrhage that caused death. Asked to speculate, however, he came up with the theory that a blow struck with the iron bar found in the house had caused the fatal injury.

The jurors were asked to avoid the "natural prejudice" felt towards a man accused of killing a child. They retired at 7.45 pm and returned forty-five minutes later with a guilty verdict. The defence, with some justification, considered that Richard Justin hadn't been given the benefit of what appeared to be a reasonable doubt. There was a possibility, it was felt, the jury had believed him guilty of scheming to kill the child, and that the plot had not succeeded only because of an unfortunate accident. In other words, even if he hadn't actually murdered Annie, there was no reason to consider him innocent when he had an evil intent towards the girl. A petition sent to the Lord Lieutenant asking for a reprieve was turned down, and Richard Justin was left to face his last days in the condemned cell at Crumlin Road.

The execution was carried out on 19 August 1909, apparently without any unusual incidents. The Rev Frederick Woolley, of the Unitarian Mission on Belfast's Stanhope Street, shared Justin's last few hours, reading him prayers and offering solace up until the release of the gallows' trap doors a few seconds after 8.00 am. A fair size crowd had gathered outside the prison, filling the Crumlin Road between the gaol and courthouse. There was even less for them to see than at previous executions, however, for the custom of hoisting a black flag immediately the condemned man was pronounced dead had been abandoned in the intervening years since Woods' execution. The prison bell was still rung and was still tolling when a warder appeared at the doors to nail up a notice, signed by High Sheriff Francis Curley, Under Sheriff James Quail, Thomas Stringer the Governor and Mr Woolley stating the "judgment of death" had been carried out. A certificate of death, signed by Dr John Stewart, the prison doctor, was also posted. An inquest, opened by city coroner Dr James Graham at 10.00 am in the Governor's room at the gaol, heard that Justin had walked firmly to the scaffold and had shown great remorse for his crime. Death, Dr Stewart assured the jurors, had been instantaneous. A few hours later Justin's body joined the others alongside the graveyard wall.

CHAPTER TEN

Troubled times

*God was good to you, for if you had been near the premises
you would have been shot too.*

Murderer William Smiley

Execution of Simon McGeown

19 August 1922

Fᴏʀ ᴅᴀʏs Rᴏʙᴇʀᴛ Fᴜʟʟᴇʀᴛᴏɴ walked the streets of north Belfast in the vain hope he would find his seven-year-old daughter. With every passing hour, and the fruitless searches of entries and empty houses, his distress had grown more acute. Maggie was a good girl and he knew she wouldn't just wander off like that. Fullerton called on neighbours, asking if they had seen the child. He talked to her friends and he regularly checked with the police in case they had news. But for four days there was nothing. In his heart the father knew he would never see his little girl alive again. Then came the knock at his door he had feared the most. Maggie was dead, the victim of a paedophile.

It was on the Tuesday evening of 30 May 1922, about 6.00 pm, that Fullerton had last seen her alive at the family's Little Henry Street home. He had given her two pennies to buy sweets from the corner shop. An hour later, when he went out to bring her in for the night, she was nowhere to be seen. It wasn't until the Saturday that the distressed father was to set eyes on his daughter again, when he identified her battered and bloodied corpse as it lay on a morgue dissecting table. The body had been found by Samuel Armstrong,

The grounds of Belfast Castle, seen in the distance just right of centre in this photograph taken from the Cavehill Road, where the body of seven-year-old Maggie Fullerton was discovered. *(Courtesy of the National Library of Ireland)*

a gamekeeper working for Lord Shaftesbury on his Cave Hill estate. He had been in the pine plantation that morning, accompanied by his faithful hound, hoping to kill a hawk that was preying on small birds in the area. However, when he called the dog to his side it refused to come. Puzzled by the animal's unusual behaviour, he went to investigate and immediately spotted the cause of the dog's reluctance. Beneath a pile of rubbish and leaves was a child's body, with the feet clearly visible. Within an hour the plantation was swarming with policemen and the hunt for the killer was underway.

A few days later, on 7 June, Belfast City Coroner Dr J Graham held an inquest into the death. It was a harrowing tale. The doctor who had carried out the postmortem gave details of his findings. The little seven-year-old, he told a hushed court, had been brutally raped and then savagely battered and stabbed. There was a gaping wound measuring two inches by an inch to her abdomen and her skull was fractured in several places, either as a result of being repeatedly kicked or being struck with a blunt instrument, with these latter injuries being the cause of death. In addition, her body was covered in a mass of bruises and fingernail scratches. The corpse had also attracted the

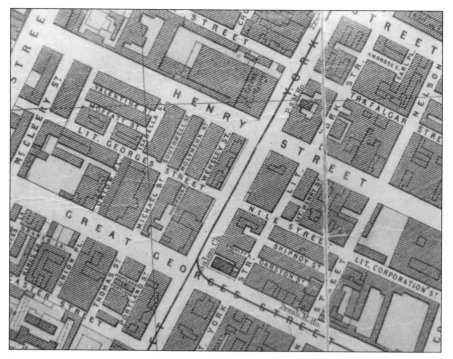

The Ordnance Survey map of 1888 shows the area around Henry Street where Maggie Fullerton was lured away by McGeown towards York Street at the top left.

attentions of the estate's wildlife, with the left foot badly gnawed by rats and the eyes and part of the forehead eaten away by field maggots. The inquest recorded a verdict of "murder by some unknown person," but it was a mystery the police were already well on their way to solving. Within 24 hours of the inquest closing, a 38-year-old man named Simon McGeown, who was already being held in police custody on another charge, was positively identified by three witnesses as having been with Maggie on the day of her disappearance.

Born near Lurgan, McGeown had joined the army as a young man and was soon drafted to India, where he served with distinction until struck down in quick succession by sunstroke, malaria and intestine problems. His military career went rapidly downhill thereafter, and he regularly found himself before his superiors on a variety of petty charges. Discharged from the army, he returned to Northern Ireland but had difficulty settling back into civilian life. The start of the First World War, in August 1914, gave him the opportunity to re-enlist, which he did within a week. With his previous training to his credit, McGeown was rapidly processed and on a boat to France to help stabilise the British lines. Wounded at least twice, and suffering the effects of gas attacks, he was discharged from the army as unfit to serve and again found himself back in Ireland without a job or prospects. Over the next few years he was to be arrested and charged on half-a-dozen occasions for a range of offences, including breaking and entering, larceny and receiving stolen goods. In total, he had spent some thirty months in gaol up until being charged with Maggie's murder.

On 22 July, some six weeks after being charged, McGeown took his place in the dock of the Belfast City Commission before Lord Justice Andrews. His trial was to take just one day. The former soldier stood rigidly to attention when asked to plead. Described in the newspapers as a "strong muscular-looking man," he attempted to put in as respectable an appearance as possible. His black hair was well brushed, and he was dressed in a grey suit and shirt, though without a collar or tie. The court heard how McGeown, who had been staying in a lodging house in Henry Street at the time of the murder, was constantly in trouble with the law. An alcoholic, he had spent most of 30 May, the day of Maggie's disappearance, drinking methylated spirits. His thirst, no doubt, had increased on hearing police officers had called at his lodgings asking about him. McGeown decided to move on. A 13-year-old girl, Annie Addis, of Ellen's Court on Nile Street, told how McGeown had approached her and a friend about 6.30 pm that evening and asked her to go with him to collect clothes from a woman on the Limestone Road. McGeown had told her the woman wouldn't part with the items unless "his little girl" accompanied him. Annie insisted she ask her mother first, and ran home. Ten minutes later, when she came back, she saw McGeown with Maggie Fullerton in Henry Street. The girl was holding his hand as they walked towards his lodging house to collect his belongings. The two then strolled along Henry Street towards York Street. A second girl, Maggie Larkham, who lived close to the murdered child in Little Henry Street, also saw the pair walking towards York Street. She called out, "Come on back out of that, Maggie," but the girl just looked round and laughed.

At 7.00 pm, the all-male jury (women had been asked to 'stand by' because of the distressing nature of the evidence) retired to make their judgment. Less than an hour later they returned with a guilty verdict. Asked if he had anything to say before the sentence of death was passed, McGeown could only manage to whisper, "I have nothing to say, sir." The judge donned the black cap and set the execution date for 17 August. McGeown was the first man to face the gallows in the newly formed State of Northern Ireland and as such the issue of whether or not a reprieve was in order came before the Cabinet at a meeting in Stormont Castle on Wednesday, 9 August 1922. Among those

BRUTAL BELFAST MURDER.

CHILD'S TERRIBLE DEATH.

Girl's Story of Mysterious Man.

GRUESOME DISCOVERY ON CAVE HILL.

The Coroner (Dr. Graham) held an inquest yesterday regarding the circumstances which led to the death of Maggie Fullerton, aged 7, whose parents live at 48, Little York Street. Head-Constable M'Kenzie conducted the examination of witnesses.

The father said the child left home about six o'clock on the night of the 30th ult., and did not return. He reported her disappearance to the police at Henry Street, and did not see her again until he was brought to the Morgue to view the body.

Annie Addis, a schoolgirl residing in Ellen's Court, Nile Street, said that on the evening of 30th May she was standing in Henry Street with another girl when a man came over and asked her to go with him to a cellar in a house on the Limestone Road. He said he had some clothes there, but "the woman would not give them to him unless his wee girl went with him for them." He explained that she would have to go down into the cellar, and when she got the clothes she could run home with them. Witness told the man that she could not go with him until she asked her mother. He said, "There is no call to ask your mother." She then ran away from the man, whom she saw about ten minutes afterwards going down to a lodging-house in Henry Street with Maggie Fullerton, the deceased, whom he left standing on the footpath while he went into the house. He came out in a few minutes with a topcoat over his arm, and took Maggie Fullerton by the arm, going up Henry Street towards York Street. They both stopped by a watchman's fire at the corner of Henry Street and York Street. Witness saw the man speak to deceased, and whatever he said to her she then walked down York Street towards the Midland Railway Station, the man following immediately behind. She would know the man again if she saw him.

A DOG'S SAGACITY.

Samuel Armstrong deposed that he was gamekeeper to Lord Shaftesbury, at Belfast Castle. On June 3, about two o'clock in the afternoon, he went to the Pine Plantation to look for a hawk that had been killing the young birds. He called to his dog, which was with him, but it refused to come, and, as this was unusual, he went over to where the animal was, and saw the two feet of a child sticking out from some rubbish. He thought there was a dead body there, and immediately sent his son with the information to Chichester Road Police Barracks. Sergeant M——

Simon McGeown, a former soldier who had served during the First World War, was convicted of the murder of a little girl. *(Belfast Telegraph)*

Report in the *Northern Whig* on the inquest into the death of Maggie Fullerton, sexually assaulted and murdered in the Belfast Castle estate by Simon McGeown.

present were Prime Minister Sir James Craig, Minister of Home Affairs Sir Richard Dawson, the Minister of Labour John Miller Andrews and the Minister of Education, the Marquis of Londonderry. The Inspector General of the Royal Ulster Constabulary, Charles Wickham, was also present. The minutes of meeting read:

> "The Cabinet decided to communicate to the Lord Lieutenant the circumstances of the case of Simon McGeown although no petition against sentence had been forwarded. The recommendation of the Cabinet was that there were no circumstances in the case which warranted mitigation of the sentence."

By 7.30 am on 17 August the bulk of more than 2,000 people who were to gather outside the gaol had already taken up position. Most were women and children, though a substantial number of men stopped off on their way to work. There was little for them to see until a warder appeared shortly after 8.00 am to post a notice declaring the execution had taken place. At that point the police, who had held the crowd away from the prison doors, stood back to allow the sign to be read. In the crush to get into the narrow passageway, a number of people were slightly injured and the shrieks of terrified women and girls could be heard across the Crumlin Road. McGeown had reportedly went to his death with apparently the "unflinching demeanour which he had manifested at his trial," much to the relief of his executioner, Ellis, who was assisted by Willis. McGeown had freely admitted his guilt to warders, though in the same breath claimed to remember nothing of what he was alleged to have done. At 10.00 am, an inquest was held within the gaol and shortly afterwards the body of Simon McGeown was lowered into an unmarked grave.

* * *

Execution of Michael Pratley

8 May 1924

NELSON LEECH WAS A man who took his responsibilities very seriously, even to the point of being prepared to lay down his life rather than give up his employer's money. A bookkeeper at Messrs Purdy and Millard's sculptor works on College Square North, Belfast, it was his job to collect

The Purdy and Millard offices where Nelson Leech was gunned down by a gang that included Michael Pratley. *(Belfast Telegraph)*

the cash from the bank every Friday so the wage packets, handed out on Saturday morning, could be prepared. It was an important task that only an experienced and trusted man would be allowed to do, and so it was with a sense of pride that Mr Leech, brother-in-law of one of the directors, ran his weekly errand. On 7 March 1924, he set off as usual to the Ulster Bank offices in nearby Queen Street, returning a short time later with a bag of notes and small change.

But that particular Friday was far from usual. He had only just returned to his office when the doors were thrown open and three men, wearing masks and carrying guns, burst in. They demanded the staff raise their hands but Mr Leech, far from obeying, ordered the men out of the office before running to a telephone box in the room to summon help. The raiders were now in a dilemma. What had started out as a straightforward wages snatch was descending into farce with the distinct possibility that the alarm was going to be raised before they got to lay a finger on any cash. They had to think quickly and on their feet. Either they turned and ran empty-handed, or they took action. Unfortunately they choose the latter. One of the raiders fired a warning shot over Mr Leech's head, but he continued into the phone

The office at Purdy and Millard where manager Nelson Leech was shot and fatally wounded. *(Belfast Telegraph)*

box and picked up the receiver. A second man tried to pull him out and a scuffle developed. Mr Leech grabbed for the gun but missed – and suffered the consequences. From a range of less than six inches the gunman fired. The farce had become a tragedy, and all three raiders took to their heels.

While Alexander Briggs, a company clerk, ran to the shot man's aid, another employee, Miss Elizabeth Allen, gave chase. The trio had split up, two running down Galway Street and another along Hamill Street. It looked like they were going to make good their getaway, but Miss Allen had other ideas. Reaching College Square barracks she called out to Constable Francis Morteshed, who took up the chase helped by a passer-by who pointed out to him the direction the gang had taken. As the policeman reached Durham Street, he spotted two men heading into Barrack Street, one lagging behind the other. Halfway along, Constable Morteshed caught hold of the slower man, dragging him to a stop. But far from giving up, his captive whipped round and shoved the barrel of a revolver into the policeman's chest and pulled the trigger – but the gun failed to fire and he was ultimately disarmed and detained.

The arrested man was 30-year-old Michael Pratley, from Moira Street in the city. A former soldier, he had lost a leg during the Great War and no doubt it was this handicap that had impeded his escape. His weapon was found to have been one of those used in the raid, while a search of his house revealed a second revolver. Pratley admitted his part in the attempted robbery, enough in itself to convict him of murder regardless of who fired the fatal shot. Nonetheless, when his case came to trial at the City of Belfast Commission on Thursday, 10 April 1924, he insisted he had only discharged the warning shot

Constable Francis Morteshed, who gave chase and captured Michael Pratley (the spot marked by an 'X') in Barrack Street, had a lucky escape when the gunman's gun failed to fire. *(Belfast Telegraph)*

over Mr Leech's head. No doubt he was hoping that if he could convince the court he hadn't actually done the killing, a reprieve might be forthcoming. His case, however, wasn't helped by the admission in evidence of a letter he had written to his wife, Josephine, from his prison cell. It read:

> My Dearest Joe,
> I want to say a few things which are best said now. When I stand on my trial it is not unlikely that I may be sentenced to death, and it is best to know it now, instead of coming as a shock later on. This letter is being slipped out, and it would be better to burn it in case it comes into the hands of the police. No matter how the case goes, I hope the two men who were with me will do their best for you. When the trial comes I am going to say that after the shooting I changed guns with one of the others, as his gun was too big to go in his pocket. That was how I had that particular gun.

Faced with overwhelming evidence, and the prisoner's own admission, the jury took less than thirty minutes to return a guilty verdict. Pratley paled slightly but otherwise showed little emotion. Asked if he had anything to say as to why sentence of death should not be passed, he curtly replied, "I have no more to say than I have already said."

On the face of it, Pratley was that rarity of the scaffold, a professional criminal who committed murder. There is another, much more intriguing aspect to the man, however, for two days after he was sentenced to death he had been due to appear back in the same court charged with a second murder, that of Northern Ireland MP William Twaddell, shot dead two years previously by the IRA.

At about 10.30 am on 22 May 1922, Mr Twaddell was making his way from Royal Avenue through Lower Garfield Street towards North Street. As he passed an entry a group of men stepped out onto the pavement behind him, with one firing a single round into his back. Mr Twaddell fell to his knees, then onto his face. A second member of the group stepped forward and emptied his weapon into the prostrate figure. The gang then scattered, but

The *Belfast Telegraph* photographer managed to get a shot of Michael Pratley as he was led from the Custody Court.

with both gunmen making their way along Royal Avenue towards Smithfield, firing at least one more round at a man who tried to trip one of them up.

A Captain WD Ryall, who had been a police officer in India, heard the shooting as he walked along Castle Junction. Abandoning his attaché case in a doorway, he drew out his own weapon and, spotting the gunmen coming into Royal Avenue, fired two shots in their direction before his automatic pistol jammed. At this point a Constable HH Davidson emerged from the Post Office and, seeing Capt Ryall firing at the men, he also began stalking them – though he could have had no idea just why this gun battle was in progress. His gun also jammed, however, and he was forced to give up the pursuit. One of the gunmen, claimed to be Pratley, was said to have had a limp.

In the event, Pratley was not to stand trial for Mr Twaddell's murder due to his earlier conviction. His co-accused was James Woods, from Ballyhornan, Ardglass, and an officer in the Free State army who had been interned on suspicion of terrorist involvement. He had spent spells in camps in Larne and Londonderry, but it was while in Crumlin Road Gaol that he had been picked out of an identity parade by Capt Ryall as the killer of William Twaddell.

ANOTHER BELFAST SENSATION

Member of Parliament Murdered.

SHOT DOWN IN CENTRE OF CITY.

Five More Deaths Yesterday.

The great sensation of yesterday was the murder of Councillor W. J. Twaddell, a member of the Northern Parliament, who was shot down in Garfield Street, Belfast, in close proximity to Royal Avenue, the principal thoroughfare of the city.

The crime was perpetrated about half-past ten in the morning. Two or three men were concerned in the attack, and they made their escape, notwithstanding the fact that within a narrow radius there were hundreds of people astir.

A renewal of sniping occurred in the East End, and during the day three men were mortally wounded in that area. At the Midland Railway terminus a ganger was murdered, whilst a rag-picker was killed in Duncrue Street.

An electric clock mine was found in a cable man-hole in Arthur Square. It was timed to explode at two o'clock in the afternoon, and had it not been for a timely discovery very extensive damage would have been done.

GARFIELD STREET CRIME.

Shocking Daylight Tragedy

ASSASSINS' AUDACITY.

Of the many appalling crimes which have shocked the people of Belfast during recent months, none sent a greater thrill of horror through the community than the murder of Councillor W. J. Twaddell, member of Parliament for the West division of Belfast in the Northern Parliament, which took place yesterday morning. Mr. Twaddell was proceeding to his place of business in North Street about half-past ten o'clock when he was attacked by a number of men in Lower Garfield Street and seven or eight shots fired at him. He fell to the ground mortally wounded and the assassins dashed along Garfield Street and were

EAST END SNIPING.

Three Men Shot Dead.

YORK ROAD MURDERS.

The Ballymacarrett gunmen were active about eleven o'clock yesterday morning, and shots were fired in Altcar Street and Lisbon Street. Some of the snipers came to the corner of the latter thoroughfare and fired in the direction of Albertbridge Road, a man named Thos. Boyd (25) 268 Donegall Road, being shot dead, being wounded. Both men were in a cycle agent's shop immediately opposite Lisbon Street, and Boyd, who carried on a licensed business, was hit in the head and fell dead in the doorway. Lindsay, who is a mechanic employed on the

The *News Letter* headlines tell of the daylight shooting of Stormont MP William Twaddell. Pratley was later accused of being part of the murder gang.

The case aroused great excitement and a huge crowd turned up at the court. Only the jurors, witnesses and a very select audience were admitted, however, including Major-General JJ 'Ginger' O'Connell, chief of staff of the Free State army, who wore civilian clothes to Belfast. The case, of course, rested entirely on the identification evidence against Woods (which seemed weaker than that which Pratley would have faced). Unconvinced, the jury returned a not guilty verdict, though Woods didn't walk free but back into an internment camp.

Unlike Woods, Pratley's time in prison was strictly limited. His execution had been set for Thursday, 8 May, and from the outset there had been little hope of a reprieve. The Northern Ireland Cabinet had discussed the possibility on 15 April but decided instead to confirm the sentence two weeks later. A large crowd gathered outside the prison on the appointed day and stood in near silence. A few minutes after 8.00 am, a notice was posted on the prison door informing the onlookers that the death penalty had been duly carried out. Pratley had apparently met his fate with the "stoical demeanour" with which he had approached his entire predicament. Roman Catholic chaplains did their best to comfort him in his final hours, though even they could not persuade him to take a final meal or drink. Willis was the executioner and death, according to the prison doctor, was instantaneous.

Pratley took many secrets with him to his grave inside the prison walls, including the names of his fellow gang members and details of any part he may have played in the Twaddell murder. Was he simply a professional criminal who got caught up, almost by accident, in an unplanned slaying, or a politically motivated cold-blooded killer? While the questions remain, his body no longer lies within the gaol but is one of two that was subsequently exhumed and returned to family members following the closure of the prison. His remains were easily identified because of his missing leg, and today lie in Milltown Cemetery in west Belfast.

* * *

Execution of William Smiley
8 August 1928

IT WAS EARLY AFTERNOON when Kate Murdoch eventually finished budding the potatoes in the plot close to the farmhouse. It was backbreaking work and she was glad of the opportunity to call back to the house. But the sight

The cottage where William Smiley shot dead sisters Margaret and Sarah Macauley. *(Belfast Telegraph)*

that greeted her sent Kate reeling, for on the floor lay the bodies of two women, their blood splattered all over the walls, floor and furniture of the room. Another farm hand, William Smiley, was working the horses in a field nearby and Kate ran to him for help. Re-emerging from the house, he told her, "God was good to you, for if you had been near the premises you would have been shot too." Smiley should have known, for it was he who less than an hour earlier had committed one of the most callous double murders in the history of Belfast executions.

Both Smiley and Kate, along with another labourer, Thomas McCaughan, worked for the Macauley family on the farm about two miles outside Armoy. On the day of the murders, 24 May 1928, the Macauley brothers, Andrew and Leslie, were repairing a fence some three-quarters of a mile away from the farmhouse, which was known as Mullaghduff Big. Both sisters were at home and it was the younger of the pair, 43-year-old Sarah, who left about 11.30 am to bring the men their lunch. Some 20 minutes later, Margaret Macauley called the rest of the workforce into the kitchen for their dinner. Sitting at the head of the table, Margaret kept everyone enthralled by reading extracts from the newspaper of an appeal court hearing by two men, Frederick Browne and William Kennedy, who had earlier been found guilty of the murder of Constable Gutteridge in Essex the previous September. It is hardly likely,

Sarah Macauley, one of the sisters shot dead by Smiley. *(Belfast Telegraph)*

Kate Murdoch, a labourer on the Macauley farm, made the horrific discovery of her mistresses' bodies in the kitchen of the Armoy house. *(Northern Whig)*

though, that the men's predicament spurred Smiley on to hatch his own ill-conceived plan, for they too ended on the gallows.

Both men left the house at 12.20 pm, with McCaughan heading home shortly afterwards. Smiley, who initially went to the stables to prepare the horses to continue the ploughing, then went back to the house. On the kitchen wall was a shotgun that he lifted down, loaded, and turned on 48-year-old Margaret, blasting her in the head. Smiley then raided the bedrooms, taking £30 in cash, a gold watch and chain, and some silver. Sarah, meanwhile, was on her way back to the house and had met Kate on the road. The two women walked down together chatting, before separating at the door shortly before 1.00 pm. Once inside, Sarah is believed to have run to where her sister's body lay, and was leaning over her when Smiley shot her from close range, virtually blasting her head off her shoulders. Kate, heading back to the potato field, heard the shot but thought nothing of it until she discovered the bodies a short time later.

Smiley, keeping up the pretence, walked to Armoy to notify the police about the murders, before retiring to Devlin's pub for a glass of whiskey, which he paid for with one of the half crowns he had just stolen. Fortified by the drink, he returned to the farm and crossed the fields to tell the brothers that their sisters had been murdered, "You are sitting there, and the two girls shot and the gun lying across them and the house raided," he told them. It is unlikely the police would have looked much further than Smiley, a former soldier with the Royal Irish Rifles, as a suspect even in the normal course of events. His loose tongue, however, soon brought about his downfall. Within earshot of a policeman guarding the entrance of the house, in which the bodies still lay, 28-year-old Smiley and his wife had an argument. "The whole countryside say you did this thing," she challenged him. "I had nothing to do with the murder, I only took the money," he replied. "I might as well have something as the rest of them. They can do nothing but swing me, anyway." Smiley was arrested the next day, and the money found hidden in the sole of his boot. He readily admitted the theft, though maintained he wasn't the killer.

The case came to trial on 10 July 1928, in front of a packed court. Approximately another 100 people were unable to get inside and milled about in the corridors. Standing impassively in the dock, and dressed in a blue serge suit and a white silk scarf instead of a collar and tie, the slightly built Smiley appeared to take little interest in the eleven hours of evidence presented. In the witness box he claimed he had helped Margaret (he was only charged with her murder for legal reasons) with a few chores before leaving for the fields. The last time he had seen her she was sitting by the kitchen window reading, he said. The jury retired at 8.45 pm and returned just twenty minutes later with a guilty verdict. The Lord Chief Justice, before pronouncing sentence, told Smiley:

"You gave these unfortunate women no chance – not a moment before you hurled them into eternity. The law is more merciful to you, because you will be afforded some period in which to make your peace with your Maker."

Then donning the black cap, he continued:

"I now pass upon you the dreadful sentence and judgment of this court – that is that you, William Smiley, be taken from this court to the prison from whence you came, and that on Wednesday, 8 August, you be taken to the common place of execution in the gaol in which you will have been confined, and then and there be hanged by the neck until you are dead, and that your body be buried within the walls of the prison. And may the Lord Almighty have mercy on your soul."

The Macauley family grave lies in the shade of a tree-lined pathway at Armoy Presbyterian Church. *(Author)*

As Smiley turned to leave the dock, the crowded court, the majority of who were women, stood to have a last look at the man destined for the gallows. Once in the condemned cell, he admitted his guilt and, taking the judge's advice, prepared to meet his God. On the last day of the month the Northern Ireland Cabinet approved the hanging, sealing his doom. Smiley is said to have walked the short distance from the cell to the scaffold with a smile on his lips. A crowd had began gathering outside the prison from about 7.00 am but quickly and quietly dispersed after the official notices confirming that the death sentence had been carried out were posted on the gaol door. The inquest, held in the prison at 10.00 am by the city coroner, simply concluded, "Smiley had been duly executed by being hanged by the neck until dead, as required by law."

CHAPTER ELEVEN

The bloody Thirties

I think that human beings who are not infallible ought not to choose a form of punishment which is irreparable.

**Lord Chancellor Lord Gardiner
during 1969 Lords debate on hanging**

Execution of Samuel Cushnan

8 April 1930

A s POSTMAN JAMES McCANN cycled away from Toome Post Office at 8.20 am on 16 May 1929, there could have been no inkling of what lay ahead. It was the 25-year-old's usual run, carrying letters to the rural community in and around the road to Crosskeys, some four miles away. This being a Thursday, he also had a sealed bag containing the old-age pension money for the district. The journey normally took little more than an hour, so by 10.00 am he was already thirty minutes overdue and along his route people were becoming concerned that the 'postie' hadn't been seen. Some fifteen minutes later James McCann's body was found lying in a pool of blood in a quiet, lonely walkway known as Harris' Lane. He had been shot in the neck at close range, with twelve shotgun pellets later removed from the body. All around him were scattered the letters from his bag and the pension money was missing. Within hours of the shooting a huge crowd had gathered at the top of the lane, all hoping to catch a glimpse of the body and murder scene. The local police, aided by detectives brought in from Belfast, began their investigation while

141

The tightly knit community of Toome was shocked by the murder of the village postman. *(© National Museums Northern Ireland, Collection Ulster Museum, BELUM.Y.W.01.90.1)*

forensic experts scoured the area for clues. Soon a picture began to be formed of the killing. A postmortem examination had revealed that Mr McCann had consumed a fair amount of alcohol shortly before his death, while a porter bottle half-full of poteen had been found in a hedge a short distance away. The postman, it seemed, had been lured up the laneway by a "callous, treacherous acquaintance, if not a friend". There were also reports of a farm worker named Samuel Cushnan being seen in the area shortly after the shooting. A piece of cloth found on a tree near the body was also identified as the same material as a coat Cushnan was known to wear everyday.

Postman James McCann was shot dead in a quiet country lane at Crosskeys. *(Belfast Telegraph)*

'X' marks the spot on the laneway where James McCann's body was found. A bottle of poteen was found in a hedge nearby. *(Belfast Telegraph)*

Cushnan was arrested and came to trial at the Ulster Winter Assizes in Londonderry in December 1929. But, after four days of evidence, the jury failed to agree on a verdict and a retrial was ordered at the County Antrim Spring Assizes, beginning on 5 March 1930. It also lasted four days, with the jurors locked up in the courthouse each evening. They were allowed, however, to go for a walk in the prison garden in the mornings before the court opened. Hundreds of spectators turned up on each day of the trial, thought most had to be content with milling about outside as the courtroom could not accommodate everyone.

Like many murder trials, the evidence was principally circumstantial. It was also generally weak. Two girls, for example, had seen a bike which looked like Cushnan's hidden in bushes at the end of Harris' Lane only hours after the murder. The bike, it was claimed, had been left there to aid escape, but the killer had panicked and made his getaway across the fields instead to the Toome Bridge Road. The girls, however, were unable to positively identify it as belonging to the accused man. Likewise, the tailors Crawford and Barclay, of Ballymena, who had used their only three-and-a-half yards of that particular cloth to make up a suit for a Mr Cushnan in April 1925, could tie the scrap of material found at the scene to him. They could not rule out, however, that other companies in the district had not similarly bought quantities of the same fabric. But as with Pratley some six years earlier, it was a letter written in prison that was to prove the most damaging evidence against Cushnan. Written to his brother Patrick, it read:

> Dear Brother Pat,
> I got the opportunity to drop you a line through the underground post. This letter will be posted by a trustworthy friend. If you get the scythe which I had mentioned on your last visit please let me know by putting three crosses in your next letter. Brother, the boy that will post this letter will give you a call in a day or two, so he is all right. If you like he will give you a hand to look for it. The name is James Kennedy. He will tell you a good plan to do with the scythe. As regards the money, you can remove it to a safer place if you think it is not safe where it is.

The police had not found the murder weapon. However, a search of Cushnan's home had turned up the stock of a shotgun bought by him in John Irwin's, Ballymena. The barrel was missing, allegedly stolen. It was this barrel that the 'scythe' in the letter referred to, while the money was the pension cash, claimed the prosecution. Cushnan, who was in the witness box for

Lord Chief Justice William Moore (who had donned the black cap to sentence Cushnan to death) at the opening of the assizes. *(News Letter)*

Cushnan's fate, as the *News Letter* termed it, merited little column space in the newspapers, though there was still considerable public interest with a large crowd gathering outside the gaol for the execution.

CUSHNAN'S FATE.

Toomebridge Crime Expiated in Belfast.

At eight o'clock yesterday morning Samuel Cushnan paid the penalty of the law at Belfast Prison for the murder fo James M'Cann, a rural postman, near Toomebridge, on May 16th, 1929. Pierpont was the executioner.

Large numbers of people assembled outside the prison in the drizzling rain, and some women repeated the Rosary at the hour fixed for the execution. Shortly after eight o'clock a notice, signed by Mr. J. Bristow, Sub-Sheriff, and Major A. W. Long, the prison governor, notifying that the sentence of the law had been carried out, was affixed to the prison gate by a warder.

An inquest was held in the prison at ten o'clock by Dr. James Graham, J.P., City Coroner. Dr. P. E. O'Flaherty, visiting medical officer to the prison, certified the cause of death, and, other evidence having been given, the Coroner returned a verdict of death by hanging, and expressed sympathy with the relatives.

more than three hours, claimed he had spent the entire morning of the murder working in his potato plot. Described by his own counsel as a "gullible gulpin from Ballyscullion Bog," he was continuously urged to speak up while giving his evidence. Quizzed about the letter, Cushnan said the scythe referred to was an old rusty gun, hence the name. It belonged to his brother, and he had been advised by his cell mates that it should be produced to the police. The money was cash earned from the sale of livestock, which was to go to his solicitor towards the cost of his defence.

The jury, no doubt boosted by the Lord Chief Justice the Rt Hon William Moore's parting words of, "and now, gentlemen, may God's blessing rest on your labours, and may you do your best in accordance with your oaths," took exactly sixty minutes to reach a verdict of guilty. Cushnan, "a short blue-coated figure standing immobile between two tall warders," listened impassively, his hands clasped in front of him, to the death sentence being read out before turning on his heels and leaving the dock.

The Northern Ireland Cabinet met on 31 March and confirmed the death sentence. However, there must have been misgivings for special meetings were convened on 4 and 6 April to discuss the issue again, but without producing any change of heart. Tuesday, 8 April dawned a wet and miserable day, a light drizzle falling on the large crowd that had gathered outside the prison. As 8.00 am neared, some of the women began reciting the Rosary while inside executioner Pierrepoint completed his preparations. Within seconds of the appointed hour, his work was done and Samuel Cushnan's body hung inert from the end of the Crumlin Road gallows' rope. The inquest, held at 10.00 am, expressed its sympathy to the relatives of the dead.

Execution of Thomas Dornan

31 July 1931

MURDER IS GENERALLY A private affair; an event carried out behind closed doors or on isolated laneways, well away from the public gaze. On the odd occasion that the foul deed has been perpetrated in front of others, the killer has usually made a determined attempt to escape. Thomas Dornan was an exception. After shooting dead two sisters, the second such double tragedy to come to north Antrim in less than three years, he simply strode off to his home to await the arrival of the police.

Dornan was a farmer who worked a small plot of land at Skerry East, about 12 miles north-east of Ballymena. He was, or at least had been, a respectable citizen in every way, serving as sexton of nearby Newtowncrommelin Presbyterian Church. But in December 1929 the tongues began to wag after a local girl gave birth to an illegitimate child. In due course the scandalmongers were rewarded when the girl, 18-year-old Bella Aiken, accused Dornan, who was twice her age, of being the father. To his credit, he admitted the child was his and agreed to pay Bella six shillings a week in maintenance.

But Dornan, despite his apparent good grace, was far from happy, though it was to take a further 17 months before his anger manifested itself in an orgy of hate. Early on the afternoon of 22 May 1931, Dornan had seemed in good spirits as he walked among workers cutting peat from a bog near his

The Aiken family home at Skerry East, to where James Aiken ran to raise the alarm. (Northern Whig)

James Aiken indicates the spot in the field close to his home where his two sisters were callously murdered by Thomas Dornan. *(Northern Whig)*

home. He passed the time of day with some, but not Bella, who was toiling alongside her sister, Margaret, eight years her senior. The Aikens were, as the newspapers of the day put it, "of the labouring class," and worked in the bog to supplement their meagre existence.

About half-an-hour later Dornan returned to the field, this time with a gun in his hand and apparently looking for something. He approached one of the workers, John McBurney, and asked, "Did you see any word of a white cat anywhere about?" He then went over to Bella, Margaret and another woman, Maud McCarthy, telling the last named that the "peats were not ready for castling". Taking a few more steps, Dornan stopped again and, raising the gun to his shoulder, fired at a startled Bella, hitting her in the arm. A second shot followed, and the girl threw herself across Margaret in desperation. Both women, screaming and crying, tried to get away across the field, but Dornan kept walking after them, reloading and firing. By the end he had discharged at least six shots. While everyone else scattered, James Aiken, the women's brother, came running over to see what was going on and watched in horror as Dornan fired again into the now still bodies lying in a pool of blood on top of the peat. Stopped in his tracks, James challenged Dornan, who responded by reloading his gun as if to fire on him. The young man ran off home, a distance of about a quarter-mile, to raise the alarm. Dornan, meanwhile, walked home where a neighbour, William Kelly, found him sitting at the kitchen table staring into space.

Margaret Aiken, the older sister, tried to flee across the field with Bella but Dornan followed, firing repeatedly. *(Northern Whig)*

On Wednesday, 8 July, Dornan appeared in the dock of Crumlin Road Courthouse before the Lord Chief Justice. As in the previous County Antrim double killing, he was only charged with one murder, that of Bella. Given the strength of the evidence, the only worthwhile debate could be the question of his sanity, with medical experts giving conflicting evidence. The jury took just thirty minutes to reach its verdict of guilty. Asked if he had anything to say before sentence was passed, Dornan simply stared vacantly in front of him. His trial had been the first held in Northern Ireland involving a capital offence since the creation of the Court of Criminal Appeal in April 1931. No appeal, however, was lodged against the verdict.

Only a handful of people turned up outside the gaol on the day of execution, 31 July 1931. Inside, Dornan was going through his final preparations after apparently enjoying a good night's sleep. On the previous day he had received his last visit from his wife Elizabeth and several other relatives, assuring them he was prepared to meet his fate. This resolution stayed with him in his final hours and he walked calmly to his spot under the noose for executioner Pierrepoint to quickly dispatch him. Thomas Dornan, the inquest was told later, went to the scaffold with a smile on his face. "He died happy, of that I have no doubt," the acting Presbyterian chaplain the Rev S Simms, was able to say.

Execution of Eddie Cullens
13 January 1932

O N A FRIDAY NIGHT in September 1931, a circular was issued to police stations throughout Northern Ireland. It marked the widening of the net in one of the most bizarre murders ever committed in the Province. Another nineteen days were to pass before an arrest was made, and only then after an investigation which spanned Carrickfergus, Belfast, Liverpool, Leeds and London. The notice, released some twelve hours after the discovery of a body, read:

> "At 9 am on 4th September, 1931, the body of an unknown man was found lying in a field at Seskin, West Division, Carrickfergus. The body was naked save for a lady's blue and white rubber cap, and the man appeared to have been dead about twelve hours. There were no signs of a struggle having taken place, and it is possible that the body may have been brought from a distance. There were two small wounds, believed to be gunshot wounds, one on the right temple, the other immediately below the right eye.
>
> Description – age about 35 years, height 6 feet 2 inches, clean shaven, black hair, brown eyes, high cheek bones; Roman nose, slightly turned to the right; large mouth, thick lips; very irregular teeth; slight burn-mark about two inches under the left ear; very dark, swarthy skin, muscular build; somewhat flat feet. The man is of Jewish or foreign appearance. The police are anxious to receive information respecting any man answering to the description who is missing, and will be grateful to anyone reporting the finding of any clothing."

The body had been discovered by a young farm labourer, James McCalmont, from Milvarn, Ballyclare, who was out collecting milk that Thursday morning as usual when his horse began shying and refused to go any further. Looking over the dry stone wall he spotted the partially concealed corpse, which he promptly reported to his employer, farmer John Hall, who in turn notified the police.

Two days later, on the Saturday, an inquest was convened in Carrickfergus Courthouse. Its first task was to give permission for a postmortem examination to be carried out, which was performed while preliminary evidence was heard. The doctors found the man had been shot once, the bullet entering the skull half-an-inch in front of the right ear, passing through the brain before striking the back of the head and causing a fracture. It had then ricocheted, almost

A local points out for the benefit of the camera where Musa's naked body was found.
(Northern Whig)

certainly causing the wound below the right eye. A bullet was also produced at the inquest by a police constable, who had found it in "some matter" lying on the operating table after the doctors had left! The murder weapon was later determined to have been a Walther 6.35mm (0.25 in) gun. Meanwhile, the police appeal for reports of clothes being found was quickly rewarded. A bundle of items, found in a gateway at Church Lane, central Belfast, the day after the body was discovered had been handed in. It included a blue waterproof coat, jacket and trousers, all of which had been roughly cut up.

The following Tuesday, 8 September, the body was secretly buried in Belfast by the Jewish Burial Society on the assumption that the victim was a member of the Hebrew faith. It later transpired he was actually a Muslim. In the intervening days a stream of people who were missing relatives had viewed the body in a bid to determine its identity. Without any hard evidence, and with apparently no progress being made by the Royal Ulster Constabulary, wild rumours began to circulate. There were claims the dead man was a sailor from one of the many foreign ships which called at Belfast, and had run foul of a shipmate and paid the price; others had him as one of a gang who had pulled off a series of spectacular robberies in Scotland and who had come across to Ulster to allow the heat to die down, only to have a falling out among thieves; while the more off-beat suggested the victim could

Eddie Cullens was the only Jew executed in Northern Ireland. *(Belfast Telegraph)*

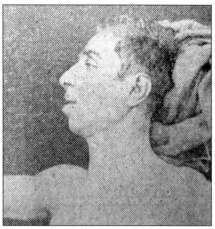

This picture of Achmet Musa, taken in the morgue, was issued to newspapers and police stations in the hope someone might be able to identify the victim. *(Belfast Telegraph)*

be a Russian Jew who had been hunted down by Soviet agents. The truth, as is so often the case, turned out to be stranger than fiction, though it wasn't until the end of September, and following the detention of a man in Gerald Road Police Station, London, that the tale could be told.

The arrested man was a 28-year-old Cypriot-born American citizen named Eddie Cullens. There was now also a name for the body – Achmet Musa, a Turk. The two men had been part of a sideshow act that also included two more Turks, Zaro Agha, claimed to be the oldest man in the world at 156, and Assim Redven. Together they arrived in England in April 1931, joining the Bertram Mills' Circus the following month on its tour of the provincial towns. In August the circus arrived in Wavertree, a surburb of Liverpool, where Cullens hired a furnished house and lock-up garage under an assumed name. It was to be later claimed in court that Cullens' intention had been to murder Musa and bury him under the garage floor. This scheme, however, came unstuck because the property owner paid too much attention to his activities.

On 28 August 1931, Cullens and Musa travelled to Belfast on the Liverpool ferry, having borrowed a car from Redven for the trip. Arriving next morning, they soon found accommodation at a boarding house on Donegall Quay run by a Matthew Ryan and his wife. Despite being an odd couple, the showmen appeared determined to enjoy themselves in a packed few days in Ireland. Musa, tall and well-built, was a married man with a wife and 15-year-old son back in Turkey. A former soldier who saw action during the First World War, he was said to be a considerable womaniser despite barely speaking a word of English. Cullens, on the other hand, was short and stocky. He had spent much of his younger days in Turkey before moving to America when he was sixteen. He lived in New York for five years, working as a film projectionist. A smart dresser, he was also, it appears, something of a ladies' man.

On the Saturday afternoon, only hours after arriving in Belfast, they met a girl named Rose McGoldrick outside the Great Northern Railway station in the city centre. After chatting to her for a while, they left her home, arranging to meet again outside the General Post Office. The next day the pair took Rose and a friend, Peggy Murphy, to Bangor for the day. On the way Cullens, who was Jewish, joked about trying to get Musa to pay for tea "but he was like a Jew

Both Cullens and his victim Musa had been part of a sideshow touring with the Bertram Mills' Circus.

and would not part with his money". More importantly, Rose was later to claim in court that at one point during the day a woman's blue and white bathing cap, similar to that found on Musa's corpse, had fallen out of the car's glove compartment. Cullens quickly put it back.

On the Monday the two men took Rose to Londonderry, but left again without her after she failed to arrive at the rendezvous point on time. The pair spent most of the next day away as well, returning to the boarding house about 6.00 pm. Later that evening Cullens offered to take the Ryans for a spin in the car, but was involved in a collision with a tram and had to leave the vehicle in for repair. On Wednesday, 2 September, he and Musa left the Ryans' house for the last time. They gave Matthew Ryan a lift into town – he was on his way to Celtic Park for the greyhound racing – dropping him off at the Albert Clock before driving up Corporation Street. Twenty-four hours later, Cullens arrived at the Belfast to Liverpool ferry terminal alone. What exactly had happened in the meantime will never be known.

Back in England, Cullens told his circus colleagues, who by then were in

Eddie Cullens being driven from a shed alongside the Liverpool ferry after being returned to Northern Ireland to stand trial. *(News Letter)*

Leeds, that Musa had met a rich woman in Londonderry and was having a great time in Ireland. He even claimed to have received a postcard from the dead Turk. The illusion was cruelly shattered, however, with the arrival of two CID officers from Belfast armed with a picture of Musa taken after death.

Cullens was tried at the Ulster Winter Assizes, held at Armagh, in December 1931, before the Lord Chief Justice. The cost of his defence was partially met by contributions from the Province's Jewish community. The jury was told that Musa's body had been dropped into the field where it was found, probably being rolled off a two-and-a-half foot high wall that ran alongside the road. There was no evidence of a struggle or of the grass being trodden in the field, though a storm which had raged on the night of 2 September would probably have removed such telltale signs.

Damning evidence came from James Hagan, who lived at Straidnahanna, two miles from Carrickfergus. He had been returning home late on 2 September when he came across an Essex saloon car, similar to the one on loan to Cullens, stopped in a narrow roadway about midnight. Its sidelights were on and the driver, whom he later identified as the prisoner in the dock, claimed to be lost. Cullens, he said, asked him if he had room to get past and if he was on the right road to Larne. The crucial element of Mr Hagan's evidence was that it put Cullens, alone in the Essex car, less than a mile-and-a-half from the spot where Musa's body was found some 36 hours later. Cullens, when he took the witness stand, insisted he had gone to Celtic Park with Matthew Ryan, leaving Musa in the car. When they returned he had gone, he said. Cullens maintained that he had then returned with his landlord

The crowd strains to catch a glimpse of Cullens as he makes his first court appearance at Carrickfergus, where he was charged with Musa's murder. *(Northern Whig)*

to the boarding house, where he spent the night. Mr Ryan, who also alleged that Assim Redven had tried to bribe him into confirming Cullens' story when the Turk had visited the boarding house on 4 November, flatly denied his version of events. After three days of evidence, the jury retired for just 34 minutes before returning with a guilty verdict. Asked if he had anything to say why sentence should not be passed, Cullens replied, "All I can say is that when I swore on my oath yesterday that I was not guilty it was the Gospel truth," which is surely an odd turn of phrase for a Jew. The execution date was set for 29 December. That morning, however, rather than hanging from a rope in Belfast gaol, Cullens was back in court "looking in the best of health" for the opening of his appeal hearing, the first time the Criminal Appeal Act had been enacted. It was a short respite, as his appeal was dismissed and an application to the Attorney General for a certificate to carry on to the House of Lords was similarly turned down. A revised date of 13 January 1932 for the hanging remained unaltered.

Cullens' last days were spent writing letters to his family of three sisters and a brother spread across Palestine, San Francisco and New York. Throughout his imprisonment Rabbi Shachter, head of the Jewish community in Ulster, visited him regularly. After the execution he told a reporter:

"The bravery of Cullens in meeting his fate was quite beyond the imagination. Up to five minutes before his death he was busy writing notes conveying his wishes and farewells to his relatives. It was with a smiling face that he parted with everyone, repeating again and again to me that he was going to face his Maker with the full satisfaction that his hands were clean of the blood of the murdered man."

Cullens was the only Jew hanged at Belfast and possibly in Ireland as a whole. The case left many questions unanswered, including the vexed notion of a motive, though there was speculation, fueled by Cullens in his appeal, that others were involved in the plot. On the practical side, it has to be asked how a small, dapper man like Cullens managed to lift the body of Musa, 6 ft 2 ins tall and weighing 14 stone, over the wall into the field without help? And, of course, why did the corpse have a bathing cap on its head? It is unlikely we will ever know with any degree of certainty.

The community that had supported Cullens throughout his trial and imprisonment has never turned its back on him. In recent years attempts have been made to have his body exhumed from its prison grave to be reburied in a Jewish cemetery. It has proved impossible to date however, as the authorities have experienced difficulties positively identifying his remains and attempts to find relatives to claim back the body have been unsuccessful.

Musa's body was initially buried in the Jewish Cemetery at Carnmoney, on the outskirts of Belfast, in the mistaken belief he was Jewish. The remains were later disinterred and returned to his family. The Hebrew community hopes one day to be able to bury Cullens here. *(Author)*

MOVEMENTS OF CULLENS AND ACHMED MUSA IN ULSTER.

Girl Recognises Bathing Cap Found on Dead Man.

THE COURT BESIEGED.

MAGISTRATE ORDERS POLICE TO DEAL WITH DISORDERLY CROWD.

Eddie Cullens, the young Turko-American, accused of the murder of Achmed Musa, whose naked body was found at Seskin on September 4th, again appeared at a Special Court at Carrickfergus yesterday, and after a lengthy hearing was remanded until next Wednesday.

While screams arose from women crushed in the crowd which surged round the Courthouse, while thirteen of the many witnesses for the Crown gave evidence, and while a woman magistrate surveyed him through green horn-rimmed lorgnettes, Cullens sat imperturbable. He did not cross-examine any of the witnesses.

CROWN'S DRAMATIC STORY.

Outlining the Crown case, Mr. H. H. Mussen traced the movements of Musa and Cullens since they formed part of a syndicate in New York to exploit Zara Agha, the 156 years old Turk, reputed to be the oldest man in the world. He described how Musa and Cullens were supposed to have quit the circus activities of the syndicate for a more lucrative form of employment, came to Belfast in a borrowed car, and stayed at a quayside hotel. Then he went on to relate how Musa and Cullens made the acquaintance of two girls and went joy-riding with them.

SUNDAY AT THE GARAGE.

On Sunday, August 30, according to the Crown case, Cullens called at a Belfast garage to change a tyre on his way to Bangor with the two girls.

After effecting the repair he washed his hands, and took a towel from the pocket in one of the doors of the car. As he did so a woman's blue and white bathing cap fell from the pocket. The Crown alleged that this cap was the same as that found on Musa's head after death.

Mr. Mussen said that District-Inspector Lewis, of the Belfast C.I.D., had found in Cullens's suitcase the case for a .25 automatic pistol. With such a weapon Musa was believed to have been shot.

The Crown further alleged that mutilated clothing found in Church Lane, Belfast, was that of the dead man.

A newspaper report of Cullens' appearance in court at Carrickfergus gives some indication of the public interest in what was seen as a sensational case. *(Northern Whig)*

Execution of Harold Courtney
7 April 1933

MINNIE REID ADJUSTED HER hat and pulled on her overcoat, struggling to button it across her ever-increasing bulge. It wouldn't be long now, she thought, before the baby was to be born. And just as certainly, she knew, she was soon to lose her refuge at the Portadown home of David Collen. The Collens had already decided to close up the house on Stewart Avenue, leaving Minnie with neither a job nor a place to stay. The problem was weighing heavily on her mind on that July night in 1932. Without a husband to explain her condition, she was too scared and ashamed to return to her parents. Picking up the tray holding her master's supper, Minnie left the scullery and made her way to the living quarters. Although it was an hour earlier than the usual meal time, the Collens made no comment for it was obvious the housemaid intended heading out that night. Within minutes she had gone, never to be seen alive again.

A week later, Minnie Reid's body was found among thick laurels in the grounds of the Verner's Estate, close to Symington's Lane and about eight miles away from the Collen house. Her throat had been cut, leaving a gaping five inch wound, and her clothes and the surrounding ground were thickly covered in congealed blood. The body was lying on its back, with the clothes and feet drawn up, though there was no sign of sexual assault. Indeed, there was no true evidence that she had even been murdered, as opposed to having taken her own life. Several days after the body was found, and following the painstaking clearance of the bushes by the police, a bloodstained razor was found some 13 feet away from where the corpse had been lying.

From the police investigation that followed there emerged a prime suspect by the name of Harold Courtney, a 23-year-old driver from Dungannon. Courtney was something of a ladies' man, always carrying on in their presence and running around with a host of different girls. His friendship with Minnie went back a long way, and had included finding her a job in Langland's Hotel, literally on his own doorstep in Dungannon. Letters found in Minnie's room after she died showed the pair had been writing to one another for some time and had arranged to meet on several occasions. Yet, when initially interviewed by the RUC, Courtney denied having anything beyond a passing acquaintance with the girl. When eventually arrested he admitted lying, claiming he wanted to distance himself from Minnie as he was engaged to be married to Lonie Motum from Dunmurry, who was the

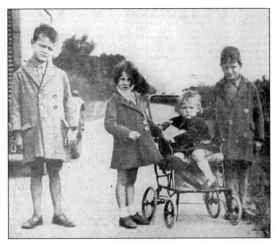

Left: The group of children that found the body of Minnie Reid lying among bushes at Derryane. *(Belfast Telegraph)*

Below left: Portrait of victim Minnie Reid. (PRONI, ARM/1/2/D/18/7)

Below right: An officer indicates the spot where the body was found, close to a rarely used laneway. *(Belfast Telegraph)*

Police cut away the bushes and undergrowth from the area around where the girl's body was discovered, a search that eventually turned up a blood covered razor. *(Belfast Telegraph)*

Telegraphic Address : " HOMAFF " BELFAST.
Telephone No.—Belfast 8321.
Any reply to this communication should
be addressed :
Secretary,
　Ministry of Home Affairs,
　　Stormont, Belfast,
　　　Northern Ireland,
and the following reference number quoted—
Ref. No. ...............M.S.3471.................

Ministry of Home Affairs,
Stormont,
Belfast,
Northern Ireland.

5th April, 1933.

Sir,

   I am directed to inform you that petitions on
behalf of HAROLD COURTNEY, a prisoner in Belfast
Prison under sentence of death, have been duly
considered by the Cabinet, who have failed to
discover any grounds which would justify them in
advising His Grace the Governor of Northern Ireland
to interfere with the due course of law.

   His Grace has, accordingly, decided that the
law must take its course.

       I am, Sir,
        Your obedient Servant,

       Stanfield

      Asst. SECRETARY.

Valentine Wilson, Esq.,
 Under Sheriff for County Armagh,
  ARMAGH.

LW.

The prison Governor, who in practice bore most of the responsibility for ensuring the execution was carried out properly once the hangman arrived at the gaol, was kept informed of the arrangements being made by the Under Sheriff. *(PRONI, D1523/2)*

"jealous type". Indeed, the pair had been due to wed on 21 September 1932, less than two months after Minnie's death.

The jury was unable to agree a verdict at Courtney's first trial at Downpatrick in December, and so the final scene came to be played out at Armagh Courthouse in March 1933. There was still the crucial question to be answered: had a murder been committed or was Minnie Reid's death suicide. Both sides called two eminent doctors each, who took fundamentally opposing views. For the Crown, pathologist Professor John Young and Dr George Dougan conceded it might have been suicide, but considered it more likely to have been murder. Likewise for the defence, Belfast surgeon TS Kirk and Dr MT Whitla, from Monaghan, admitted the wound could have been caused by an assailant, but thought it more likely the girl had taken her own life. The strongest argument in the suicide theory was the fact that Minnie would not have lost consciousness for several minutes after the wound had been inflicted, yet had made no effort to move or get up, simply sitting there waiting for death. Despite the conflicting evidence, the Attorney General entertained no such doubts. He told the court,

> "I say that the prisoner, and the prisoner alone, stands in the centre of the evidence and that every thread leads directly to him; I say it is as clear as a sign-post on a main road; I say no other person could fill the position as prisoner does."

Courtney, the court was told, had in all probability fathered the child Minnie had been expecting and had wanted to silence her. While the evidence against him was circumstantial, it quickly mounted up. A park keeper claimed he had seen the pair together at Donaghmore in June 1932; a taxi driver told the court he had taken a woman answering Minnie's description to Verner's Estate on 25 July to meet someone; a railway porter said Courtney had called at Vernersbridge Station on 26 July looking to meet someone off the train. On the night of Minnie's disappearance Courtney had hired a car from Robert Ardery, driving off in it at 8.00 pm and returning about 10.15 pm. He claimed to have used it to go to Armagh in search of a man who had offered him a better-paid job. However, 13-year-old Olive Symington reported seeing a similar car parked in a laneway close to the murder scene about 9.00 pm that evening. After five days of evidence, the jury retired for little more than an hour before returning to the courtroom. The News Letter reported:

> "Courtney retained his composure to the end. Anxiety, however, was clearly written on his countenance as the jury slowly filed back into court after an hour and a quarter of deliberation. The ashen grey of the faces of some of them indicated to the observant the momentous decision at which they had arrived. The prisoner stood between warders in the dock, raising and lowering himself ever so slightly on his toes, his chest rising and falling with emotion. It was his first outward sign of anxiety in the five days."

The execution of Courtney was the second overseen by Prison Governor Captain Thomas Moore Stuart. He was also in charge when Eddie Cullens, and later Tom Williams, were hanged. *(Belfast Telegraph)*

Along with the guilty verdict, the jury included a strong recommendation for mercy. The Lord Chief Justice, however, immediately poured cold water on any hopes of a reprieve that Courtney might have been entertaining:

> Harold Courtney, a jury of your fellow countrymen have brought in a verdict with which I cordially agree, and every reasonably thinking man in the court would, I think, arrive at the same conclusion. It is my duty out of respect to the jury to forward their recommendation of mercy to the proper authorities, but in doing so it is only fair that I should tell you that I profoundly disagree with it. I think it was a cold blooded, calculated and callous murder. I think you betrayed this girl; under the stress of her claims upon you, you butchered her and her unborn child. I may tell you – it is only fair to tell you – that so far as I am concerned I can hold out no hope that the sentence will not be carried out.

The execution date was set for Friday, 7 April 1932, and remained unchanged. A crowd began gathering outside the prison gates from early on, eventually growing large enough to block traffic for a while. A few seconds after 8.00 am, Pierrepoint, the executioner, pushed the lever and Harold Courtney dropped to his death. Two hours later the formalities were completed when the inquest returned a verdict of lawful execution and Courtney's remains joined those of the other murderers who had breathed their last in the gaol.

CHAPTER TWELVE

For the sake of Ireland

Many of us remember the time, not all that long ago, when human life was prized in this land and when a murder was talked about, in horror, for months.

**Former Presbyterian Moderator Dr John Dunlop
at the 1992 funeral of a murdered RUC officer**

Execution of Thomas Williams

2 September 1942

GIVEN NORTHERN IRELAND'S TROUBLED history, it is perhaps surprising that only one terrorist has been hanged on the Belfast gallows. That dubious distinction belongs to Thomas Joseph Williams, who was executed in Crumlin Road Gaol on 2 September 1942, one of six Irish Republican Army (IRA) men originally sentenced to die that day.

The Second World War had presented an opportunity to republicans to step up their campaign aimed at forcing the British out of Ireland. On the day war was declared there were several incidents, including shots fired at the police. It was to England, however, that the IRA turned its attentions first. A plan had been drawn up to mount a bombing campaign on the mainland. No loss of life was envisaged, rather the intention was to make the English realise the potential trouble the Irish terror group posed in the hope it would shake their resolve to maintain the Union. It was an ill-conceived policy that went tragically wrong when five people were killed in a bomb attack for which two men, Peter Barnes and Frank Richards (alias McCormick), were later executed.

South of the Irish border the police took a tough line with the IRA, with casualties mounting up on both sides, and a number of terrorists meeting their ends on the gallows. In Northern Ireland, despite isolated incidents, the republican campaign showed little sense of purpose in the early years of the war. This, in no small measure, had been due to the success of the RUC in arresting suspects in swoops prior to the outbreak of hostilities with Germany. However, in 1942 the IRA's Northern Command was sufficiently strong again to mount a campaign of its own that would ultimately claim the lives of five RUC and Special Constabulary members and result in the deaths of three terrorists, including Tom Williams.

About 3.00 pm on Easter Sunday, 1942, a four-man RUC patrol slowly drove up Clonard Gardens in Belfast, heading towards Cupar Street. As the vehicle reached the Kashmir Road junction a fusillade of shots rang out, between seven and ten rounds in total, fired by a group of five men who had been hiding behind an air raid shelter. The attack had been planned as a diversion, to draw the police into the area to allow Easter commemorations to take place without disturbance elsewhere in the city, and it had not been intended to hit the police vehicle. However, one bullet did strike home, smashing the windscreen though causing no injuries. As the gang took off, three police officers leapt from the car and gave chase into Kashmir Road and down Cawnpore Street. A house-to-house search was started, during which Constable Patrick Murphy entered 54 Cawnpore Street to be confronted by the gunmen. In an exchange of shots, the officer fell fatally wounded, his service Webley Revolver still clasped in his right hand. Shortly afterwards the police arrested six men and two girls in the bedroom of the house. One, Williams, had been wounded with two bullets in his left thigh and one in his left arm, all fired by Constable Murphy. It later emerged the officer had fired only three rounds, each finding its target, before his gun had misfired.

Constable Murphy, who had been stationed at Springfield Road barracks, had lived at Clowney Street, off the Falls Road. He left a widow and nine children. The RUC band led his funeral cortege from St Paul's Roman Catholic Church to Milltown Cemetery, with 100 colleagues, including the City Commissioner of Police and Deputy Commissioner of Police in attendance. Two months later, during a three-day Royal visit to the Province, King George VI presented his widow with her husband's Police Medal during a special ceremony at Stormont Castle. A few weeks later, on 28 July 1942, the trial of the six men – Henry Cordner, William Perry, John Oliver, Patrick Simpson, Joseph Cahill and Williams – began before Lord Justice Murphy at the Belfast City Commission. All were aged between 18 and 21. There was

IRA man Tom Williams was the only member of his gang to face the executioner. *(National Graves Association)*

little doubt of their collective guilt in the incident, though obviously some bore more responsibility than others. In a lengthy statement, given eight days after the murder from his bed in the Royal Victoria Hospital, Williams claimed that he alone had organised the attack "as a protest against the English occupying Ireland". He had armed the men and been solely responsible for Constable Murphy's death, he said. It had been previously arranged, he told police, that after the shooting the weapons – a short Webley, three Webleys and a Parabellum – would be handed over to two girls and Simpson (who, though he never had a gun, was found with nine bullets in his pockets when arrested) in an entry off Cawnpore Street. Instead of escaping with the weapons, however, the girls followed the men into the house.

> "I ran into the parlour and I heard the police knocking at the next door, the second one from Cupar Street. I then grabbed my revolver from the brown leather bag which was lying on the floor in the kitchen. This was the bag we put the revolvers into in the entry and was brought to the house by the girls. Some one of the eight persons said that a policeman was coming into the house by the entry door. I ran into the scullery. There is a little glass enclosure in the yard and from the scullery window I could see a policeman coming into this enclosure with his gun drawn.

When he was about three yards from me and beside the kitchen window I pointed my revolver at his body and fired one shot. He staggered and fired back, and I fired four or five more shots at his body. The revolver I had was re-loaded by me after it had been brought to the house by the girls. No other person in the house had fired at Constable Murphy. I then shouted that I had been shot. I dropped my revolver and heard Constable Murphy groan and fall to the ground. Constable Murphy's body was lying between the glass enclosure and the door which leads from the scullery to the kitchen. I stepped over his body and ran into the hall of the house and there I fainted. Next thing I remember – when I woke up on a bed in the back room up the stairs – some of the party I had commanded said "What do you want us to do?" I said "Where are the police" and someone answered "They have the house surrounded" and I told them to surrender, which they did. About five policemen came into the room where I was lying and they arrested us."

How the *Irish News* reported Constable Patrick Murphy's murder and the arrest of the IRA gang.

It was a gallant attempt by Williams – who described himself in a letter, smuggled out of the gaol, as a lieutenant in C Company of the IRA's Belfast brigade – to give his accomplices a chance of escaping the gallows, and was never seriously challenged in court. Besides, as the law stood if one was guilty of murder, they all were, regardless of who pulled the trigger. However, Constable Murphy was shot five times, twice in the chest and three times in the abdomen, with one bullet passing through his heart. A sixth bullet struck his gun holster. Robert Churchill, a London ballistics expert, said in evidence that four revolvers, including the constable's, had been fired in the house. Constable Murphy, he claimed, had three bullets in him from a Webley and two from a short Webley, indicating at least two gunmen. The Attorney General, in answering charges that Joe Cahill (who later went on to become the IRA's chief of staff in the early 1970s) had been severely assaulted by the arresting officers, told the court:

> "Even if, seeing his comrade lying in a pool of blood, some constable did not treat Cahill with gentle care, didn't that point in another direction from that indicated by learned counsel for the defence? Was it not a two-edged weapon? Didn't it indicate that the police regarded Cahill as being directly connected with what had happened down stairs in that house?"

The twelve-strong jury, which had taken ninety minutes to select because of almost 150 challenges by both parties, retired on the third day. It returned after two hours and five minutes with six guilty verdicts, but with a recommendation for mercy in Simpson's case because of his youth. Williams' last words to the court were, "I am not guilty of murder. I am not afraid to die. There was no premeditation." The execution date was set for 18 August, but was put back when appeal papers were lodged. Within days 60,000 people in nationalist areas had signed a petition calling for a reprieve. Forms had been available in the porches of Roman Catholic churches on the Sunday following the verdict, and priests implored their congregations to sign them. Later that afternoon schools were opened up to act as centres for the collection of signatures. When the petition was finally handed in to the Stormont Minister of Home Affairs on 22 August, it had almost 200,000 names on it. Telegrams asking for support had also been sent across the world to influential people, including American President Franklin D Roosevelt, British Prime Minister Winston Churchill, Home Secretary Herbert Morrison and several Irish-American groups. Nationalist members of the Northern Ireland Parliament and Senate appealed directly to the Governor of Northern Ireland to save the men, "With a deep sense of our responsibility, we plead for mercy towards

Irish president Eamonn De Valera received delegations, including one led by union leader James Larkin, urging his help in having the death sentences commuted. (News Letter)

them," they wrote. "We submit to your judgment that the exercise of mercy would satisfy the ends of justice, and allay anxiety and apprehension agitating many minds about their fate." A Dublin Reprieve Committee was formed and was widely supported by both the public and political figures south of the border. Taoiseach Éamon de Valera met a number of delegations urging his support, including one from union leader James Larkin.

The Court of Appeal sat on Wednesday and Thursday, 19 and 20 August 1942, the verdict that the convictions must stand being delivered the next day. A new date of 2 September was fixed for the hangings. Leave to appeal to the House of Lords was lodged on 26 August but refused by the Attorney General. The following day a conference in the Mansion House, Dublin, called on the people of Ireland to make the day of execution one of national mourning. The resolution said the conference,

> "conscious of the deep feeling that the execution of any of the six men would arouse, urges the Irish people to show the utmost restraint, and to make it known to the world that any such execution had not the sanction of the Irish people".

The Northern Ireland Cabinet discussed the death sentences, and the possible unrest that would follow the executions, at length on 26, 27 and 29 August. The next day, Sunday, 30 August, a statement was issued on behalf of the Governor of Northern Ireland. It read:

> His Grace the Governor of Northern Ireland has considered the cases of Thomas Joseph Williams, William J Perry, Henry Cordner, John Terence Oliver, Joseph Cahill and Patrick Simpson, prisoners lying under sentence of death in H.M. Prison, Belfast, and has decided:
> That in the case of Thomas Joseph Williams the law must take its own course; That in the case of William J. Perry, Henry Cordner, John T. Oliver and Joseph Cahill sentence of death shall be commuted to one of penal servitude for life; and that in the case of Patrick Simpson sentence of death shall be commuted to penal servitude for 15 years.

The news was given to the men by their solicitor, with the others taking it in turn to embrace Williams, who apparently showed no emotion but told them, "Don't worry about me. I am all right. I am fully prepared to die." As word spread of the reprieves, cheering crowds gathered outside the homes of the men. Dublin's Lord Mayor, Alderman PS Doyle, arrived in Belfast the day after the Governor's statement and in the wake of a telegram sent to his Belfast counterpart which read:

> Corporation of Dublin in special meeting assembled unanimously adopted the following resolution: That the Corporation of the City of Dublin gives its fullest support to the appeal for the reprieve of the six young men awaiting execution in Belfast Prison. In view of the good relationship which exists between the two corporations, I earnestly request you to exercise your good offices in the matter.

Before treating Mr Doyle to lunch in the City Hall, followed by private meetings, the Belfast Councillors had already formulated their reply:

> Resolved: That this Council appreciate the reference to the good relationship existing between the two bodies and the motives which prompted the request but they feel that as the subject has already been dealt with by His Grace the Governor of Northern Ireland, action on their part is not called for.

At 8.00 am on 2 September 1942, 19-year-old Tom Williams walked the short distance from the condemned cell to the gallows at the beginning of a day of violence and protest throughout Ireland. The RUC was well aware of the risk of violence. Two days earlier another IRA man, moving arms in preparation for revenge attacks for Williams' execution, had been shot dead at Hannahstown. On the eve of the hanging, a crowd had gathered outside the gaol, catching the police unaware. The following morning, in a bid to frustrate similar scenes, a large area around the prison was cordoned off, with patrol cars and tenders much in evidence on the streets. The Crumlin Road was closed from Carlisle Circus to Agnes Street, forcing vehicles and pedestrians to make diversions. Tramcars, carrying workers on their way to the mills and factories, were the only vehicles allowed past the prison, and only then on the condition they didn't stop. Those living in the restricted area could only pass the gaol after producing their identity cards to police. Inside the prison Williams had celebrated Mass at 6.35 am and again at 7.15 am. He is said to have joined in the prayers as the prison chaplain, the Rev Patrick McAlister, led him to the scaffold. The previous evening he had been visited by his brother Richard, who was serving with the Irish army's Air Corps, his elderly grandmother, Mary Fay, with whom he had lived, and an uncle, Charles Fay. Williams also received a telegram from his father, also serving in the Irish army. It read, "Be brave to the end, my son. Goodbye, and God bless you."

Outside the police cordon on the Crumlin Road people gathered on the pavement, with many of the women offering up prayers for the soul of the teenager. A rival faction had taken up position on the opposite side of the street, and as the appointed time of execution drew closer the tension threatened to spill over. The *News Letter* reported:

"Police had to intervene at the corner of Old Lodge Road and Florence Place, which runs alongside the County Courthouse. Here on the stroke of eight, a crowd of about 200 women and girls burst into 'God Save the King', while on the other side of the street a score of women were kneeling. Cheers followed the National Anthem, and then the crowd sang 'Land of Hope and Glory' and 'There'll Always Be An England', the praying women meanwhile remaining on their knees."

Police eventually managed to restore order, gradually forcing the singing women back into a side street, with one woman calling out, "There are men being killed at the Front every day, and they don't pray for them." At 8.05 am the official notice that the execution had been carried out, signed by the Under Sheriff of Belfast, Robert Henderson, a Justice of the Peace, George Stewart, prison Governor Captain Thomas Moore Stuart, and the prison chaplain was nailed to the gaol's main door. The police then withdrew, allowing the bulk of

A republican memorial in Milltown Cemetery, known as the old Fenian monument, carries Tom Williams' name. Alongside it, out of camera shot, is the County Antrim monument, where a grave had been reserved for the IRA man. (Author)

the crowd that had gathered at the Carlisle Circus end of the cordon to move off towards the city centre. Some women remained, however, praying at the spot for a further half-an-hour. Marshalled by police, the protestors passed through Royal Avenue shouting and singing, with some giving Nazi salutes, and on to the Falls Road. At one stage the RUC officers were pelted with stones and bottles, and two men were arrested. They were later charged with striking a Head Constable and riotous behaviour, with each sentenced to a total of three months imprisonment.

An inquest on Williams was opened at 11.00 am, with all the jurors inspecting the body. A short funeral service, officiated by three priests, was held at noon. Present were the prison Governor and a number of Roman Catholic warders, who stood rigidly to attention as the coffin was lowered into the ground. The rest of the day was marked by protests and disturbances in Roman Catholic areas. On the Falls Road a flag-waving crowd marched down to Bombay Street, where Williams had lived, singing republican songs along the way. After holding a short silent vigil outside his home, they dispersed again. Elsewhere, black flags appeared in nationalist areas; Roman Catholic dockers in Belfast, Londonderry and Newry walked out; and police and soldiers, including the American forces, were insulted and occasionally attacked with missiles. In Dublin, many businesses closed for an hour and flags were flown at half-mast. Protestors forced buses to turn back in the city centre and several of the shops which remained open, including Easons in Sackville Street, had their windows smashed. Back in Northern Ireland, a car and lorry full of armed IRA men crossed the border at Culloville, County Armagh, about 2.15 pm that day. A police patrol, consisting of a sergeant and constable on Customs duty, gave chase. As the RUC men rounded a corner

Joe Cahill removes the Tricolour from Tom Williams' coffin at Milltown cemetery. *(Irish News)*

Joe Cahill back in the condemned cell he once shared with Tom Williams. *(Irish News)*

they found their path blocked by the gang, which opened fire, riddling the car. The officers returned fire but were quickly overpowered. The sergeant and one of the raiders were slightly injured in the gun battle, which ended with the gang fleeing back across the border.

Williams' dying wish, it was later claimed, was to be buried in the republican plot at Milltown Cemetery and a campaign to have his body exhumed was soon underway. The National Graves Association, which registers and maintains republican burial plots, reserved a grave for Williams in the cemetery and took legal action in a bid to force the Government to release the IRA man's remains. The courts, in a judicial review, ruled the Northern Ireland Secretary of State had the power to commute the portion of the sentence that required the body to remain in an unmarked prison grave. A warrant removing this clause was signed by the Queen in August 1995, and the announcement that the body was to be exhumed was made the following month, just days after the fifty-third anniversary of Williams' execution. However, a legal argument over who was entitled to lay claim to the body, and where it should be buried, caused a further delay and it wasn't until August 1999 that the body, in the presence of several relatives, was recovered from its resting place next to the prison's garden wall. It was taken to the state pathologist for examination and DNA testing, which proved inconclusive. It was felt, however, that there was enough supporting evidence, such as age, height, weight and medical condition of the body, to believe the remains were those of the executed IRA man.

On the evening of 18 January 2000, the coffin bearing Tom Williams' remains was taken to St Paul's church on the Falls Road, Belfast, where it lay overnight. The following day a funeral service was conducted by the Rev Paddy O'Donnell during which he asked the congregation to pray for the family of constable Patrick Murphy, the officer who had died in that Easter Sunday shooting in 1942 and whose funeral had been from the same church. It would also have been known to many of those present that his grandson, John Murphy, a former RUC officer, had been murdered by the Irish National Liberation Army in a Belfast hotel half-a-century later in 1993. Among those who carried Williams' Tricolour-covered coffin to its final resting place, in a family grave rather than the republican plot, were Sinn Féin President Gerry Adams and Joe Cahill and John Oliver, two of the reprieved condemned men. The words "in proud memory of Lieut Thomas J Williams, C Coy IRA, executed 2 Sept 1942 in Belfast Prison aged 19 years" had been added to the headstone many years before. Dr Philip Williams, a half brother of Tom who had travelled from Canada, told the mourners:

"So young Tom returns to his family after a long, long time. We would like to offer thanks to the people of Clonard for their help in being here today in such a touching manner and National Graves for their unfailing spirit which has produced what has happened here today. We came here from far to see this day and would like to thank you all from the bottom of our hearts."

A commemoration was held the following Sunday, 23 January, to Milltown Cemetery from Williams' last home in Bombay Street, where Madge McConville, who as a girl had been one of those passed the guns by the gang that fateful day, laid a wreath. Canon Patrick McAllister, who attended Williams at his execution, died just weeks later in February 2000.

The headstone over the Williams' family grave, and republican veterans Madge McConville, one of those to whom the guns had been passed after shots had been fired at the police car, and Joe Cahill. *(Irish News)*

CHAPTER THIRTEEN

The curtain drops

In fifty years time this event will be looked back on with the same attitude that we now have to witch-hunting.

**Denis Barritt, of the Society of Friends,
after a 1961 execution in Belfast**

Execution of Samuel McLaughlin

25 July 1961

"I NEVER INTENDED HURTING or harming my wife. I always loved my wife," Samuel McLaughlin told the hushed courtroom moments before being sentenced to death for her murder. They were heartfelt words from a man who had quite literally destroyed his own world during a bout of jealous rage sparked by days of excessive drinking.

McLaughlin, on the face of it a normally quiet, inoffensive man, had left his native Cloughmills, in County Antrim, in 1941, aged twenty-one, to enlist in the RAF. He saw service in Belgium, France and Italy as the victorious Allied forces pressed through Europe on the heels of the retreating Germans. Once in Italy, however, his troubles began. Caught dealing on the black market, he was tried by court martial and sentenced to three years in gaol, later reduced to two years. His time behind bars was served in England and he was discharged from the services on his release from prison in 1949. On his return to Northern Ireland his luck appeared to be changing as he quickly found work driving a lorry, and romance. The latter came in the form of an

Prison Governor Lance Thompson, seen here on his daily inspection tour of the gaol with the head warder, was in charge during the last two executions in Belfast. *(Belfast Telegraph)*

old friend, Nellie Given, whom he had known as a child. Now, however, she was an attractive 21-year-old member of the Auxiliary Training Service. Their relationship blossomed, and in 1951 they married. The young couple moved to Derby, where McLaughlin had found a job in a foundry. They lived at first in a furnished flat, then a council house, and after a few years McLaughlin moved to another factory, turning out parts for lawnmowers, and seemed well settled in his new surroundings. Nellie, on the other hand, was extremely unhappy. She detested their new house, didn't get on with the neighbours and felt desperately home sick. At Christmas 1959, she could stick it no longer and moved back to stay with her mother in a two-roomed cottage at Lislaban, Cloughmills. McLaughlin, much to his disgust, was ordered to pay his wife £3 a week in maintenance. At the hearing she accused him of ill treatment and infidelity, while he countered by claiming she was "nagging and difficult".

Despite the acrimony, McLaughlin still obviously loved his wife and she apparently still felt something for him, though, as he was to tell police later, he believed she had been "playing around" since their separation. In October 1960 he took time off from the Qualcast foundry and, having two days previously signed for a new house to which he hoped to bring back his

32-year-old wife, he headed off on his motorbike to catch the boat to Ulster. Once home, he spent the next few days calling on friends and drinking in the pubs. Strangely, it wasn't until Monday, 17 October 1960, the day he had originally planned on returning to Derby, that he met up with Nellie. The reunion evidently went well, with most of that evening spent together in Richmond's pub in Cloughmills. At one stage Nellie began singing *Goodnight Irene* into her husband's face, bringing tears to his eyes. Delicately she wiped them away as McLaughlin took up the song. The couple returned, armed with a carryout of stout, whiskey and rum, to the home Nellie shared with her mother, Martha Given, and continued drinking. Later, in front of a blazing fire, they made love.

The following day, McLaughlin, Nellie and Mrs Given had lunch together before the couple set off on the motorbike to visit friends. That evening it was back to the pubs for another drinking bout. About 9.00 pm they went for a meal, returned to the pub for a last drink, then headed off to the cottage around 10.00 pm. That was the last time Nellie was seen alive. That Tuesday night the pair had the property to themselves for Mrs Given, at Nellie's request, had gone to stay with relatives. When she returned home about noon the following day she found the doors locked and the blinds drawn. Later, with still no life about the cottage, Nellie's half-sister Violet Houston alerted the police, who dispatched Special Constable Norman McIntyre. The constable, using his torch, peered through a window and spotted a body lying on the bed. He sent for Dr David Johnston Crawford, who climbed into the house through a window. Inside, he found Nellie's partially clothed body covered in blood. She had been beaten repeatedly with a broom handle, the broken remains of which lay on the floor. Death, however, had been caused by strangulation, the white nylon stocking used still tightly wrapped around her throat.

McLaughlin, soon in police custody, maintained throughout that he had no recollection of how his wife came to die, while virtually admitting in the same breath that he had killed her. During his interviews with the RUC he appeared confused and disorientated. "If I tied that stocking round her neck I may or may not have done it. I just don't know how it was done or something," was a typical response from him when quizzed.

The case was heard at the Northern Ireland Winter Assizes in February 1961, but the jury, after much wrestling with the laws covering insanity, failed to agree on a verdict. As a consequence, McLaughlin faced a retrial at the County Antrim Spring Assizes in April that year. There could be little doubt he had killed his wife but there was considerable disagreement as to his state

A warder nails the notice to the prison door confirming that Samuel McLaughlin had been duly executed for the murder of his wife. *(News Letter)*

of mind. Evidence was given by a former RAF colleague that he was prone to acts of senseless violence and memory loss when on drinking binges, though binge seems barely adequate a word to describe his intake. Between 13 and 18 October 1960, McLaughlin was estimated to have consumed daily three dozen Guinness, a half-bottle of whiskey and a half-bottle of rum. Dr John Nabney, a psychiatrist working at Purdysburn Hospital in Belfast, told the court that McLaughlin's first recollection on the day following the murder had been of finding himself up a grass lane "looking for a tree to hang himself". He was aware something terrible had happened but did not know his wife was dead, it was said. It was not a tree, however, but the gallows inside Crumlin Road Gaol that he was destined for when the jury returned with a guilty verdict after two hours and twenty minutes of deliberation. The execution date was set for 17 May, but was postponed after an appeal was lodged. The four-day hearing in the Court of Appeal, at the end of June, confirmed the original sentence and a new date set.

On the morning of 25 July 1961, 40-year-old Samuel McLaughlin joined his wife in the hereafter. The Rev AS Hoffmeester, who, as curate of St Mary's

Church of Ireland on the Crumlin Road, acted as prison chaplain and attended to McLaughlin throughout his final hours. To prepare himself for the traumatic ordeal he asked doctors for tranquillisers, an indication of just how difficult it was for everyone associated with a hanging. At 8.10 am, a notice confirming the execution had taken place was nailed to the gaol door. The heavy police presence, which included patrol cars, comfortably dealt with the one hundred or so people who had gathered outside the gates of the courthouse opposite. When they surged forward, on seeing the notice posted, they were stopped in their tracks by an RUC cordon. Denis Barritt, a member of the Society of Friends and ardent opponent of capital punishment, told a reporter outside the gates,

"In fifty years time this event will be looked back on with the same attitude that we now have to witch-hunting. Hanging is a terrible, uncivilised thing."

The crowd dispersed quietly after ten minutes when a head constable ordered them to move on. By the time executioner Harry Allen left the gaol some two hours later, it was business as usual on the Crumlin Road.

* * *

Execution of Robert McGladdery
20 December 1961

A SINGLE BLACK SHOE lay in the middle of the road. Not a remarkable occurrence on its own, but strange enough to cause Charles Ashe to stop and ponder. The 16-year-old was out early on the Old Damolly Road, outside Newry, County Down, that Saturday morning, 28 January 1961. Picking up the shoe, he examined it briefly before tossing it aside into the hedges. Carrying on towards Damolly crossroads, however, he came across other, more mystifying objects: a silk scarf in the water channel alongside the road and another in a ditch, a pair of brown shoes and the match of the black shoe. On the Belfast Road he spotted a bicycle lying in a field, just on the far side of the hedge. The abandoned bike had also been spotted by farm labourer Bob McCullough, who was putting on new gates at a field near the Upper Damolly crossroads. He and Charles passed comment on the finds before bidding farewell. About 9.30 am, McCullough left what he was doing and went off to collect a sledgehammer. What he found instead, however, filled him with dread. Scattered across the fields were items of women's clothing, some of it bloodstained. Nearby was the home of Margaret Gamble and it was to there that McCullough went for help. His arrival on her doorstep, and the news he had to tell, must have chilled Mrs Gamble to the bone. Her daughter Pearl, who had only turned nineteen four days earlier, still hadn't returned home from a dance the previous evening and she was beside herself with worry. Grabbing hold of her young daughter Eleanor, she went with McCullough to the crossroads. There she found Pearl's handbag, brush, comb, coat, belt, skirt and pants. Painfully she gathered the items up and carried them home while McCullough phoned the police. Shortly after 5.00 pm that evening, at a place known as Weir's Rocks, Pearl's body was found. She was naked, apart from her badly torn stockings, and her body had been thrown face down into bushes. Her woollen sweater, white blouse, white underskirt and bra had been thrown on top of her.

Less than an hour before the body was found, Robert Andrew McGladdery, one of a number of young men interviewed by police about Pearl's disappearance, was being quizzed in Newry RUC station. He and the girl had been friends since childhood and had danced together the previous evening. McGladdery fumed to detectives, "I wish I could get my hands on the boy that done this, you wouldn't have to deal with him." By the time the 24-year-old had left the station, however, the police officers on the case already suspected they had questioned the man responsible. Proving it, however, was another matter entirely.

The first task, of course, was to piece together as best they could what had happened in the previous twenty-four hours. Pearl, who worked as a shop assistant in Newry, had left for the dance in the Henry Thompson Memorial Orange Hall in the town with two friends, Rae Boyd and namesake, but no relation, Evelyn Gamble. They arrived there at about 10.30 pm. 'Robbie' McGladdery, accompanied by a friend, William Copeland, was not to reach the hall until almost an hour later. The young men had spent most of the day together drinking after meeting in Hollywood's pub in Hill Street. They met back there in the early evening, moving on to Magee's public house on Merchant's Quay a short time later. After brief stops at the nearby St Catherine's Club, and the Royal British Legion Club in Monaghan Street, they arrived at the Orange Hall already the worse for wear. Towards the end of the evening, McGladdery and Pearl danced together at least twice, but if he had romance in mind things obviously weren't working out. At his subsequent trial, one witness said McGladdery "was trying to hold Pearl tightly towards

Newry shop assistant Pearl Gamble, whose battered and nearly naked body was found dumped in bushes close to her home. *(News Letter)*

Robbie McGladdery, the last man to be hanged in Northern Ireland, led the police a merry dance before the evidence could be found to arrest him. *(News Letter)*

him and had his head bent down towards her face. But Pearl kept turning away from him". McGladdery, dressed in a light blue suit, then asked the band to play a popular song of the day, *It's Now or Never*, during which he stood by the doorway "wringing his hands". He left the hall shortly afterwards, not waiting for the 2.00 am finish of the dance. Pearl, meanwhile, had finished the evening with another boy. After saying goodnight to him outside, she and her two girlfriends accepted a lift, with Pearl being dropped at the Upper Damolly crossroads, close to her home. It was the last time she was seen alive by anyone but her killer.

From the injuries she sustained and the evidence at hand, it was obvious Pearl had been attacked within seconds of alighting from the car. She had been struck about the face and dragged through a gap in the hedges. Pearl, however, had put up a brave struggle from the outset and evidently continued to resist for as long as she could. Approximately 130 yards into the field, the grass was bloodied where McGladdery had tried to beat the resistance out of her. Further along, her clothes ripped from her body and possibly semiconscious, the murderer completed his brutality. A postmortem revealed a horrendous list of injuries, including a broken nose, severe bruising around the eyes and left cheek, and cuts around her lips. But these were superficial compared to the star-shaped "puncture" wounds, most about two inches deep, inflicted about the body, including near the right ear and forehead, but particularly to the chest. One had punctured the heart and would have led to death had not McGladdery finished the job by strangulation. Despite the sexual nature of the attack, she had not been raped.

McGladdery, who had raced his victim to the murder scene on a bike stolen from outside the Orange Hall, now made his way home to dispose of his bloodstained clothes. Next morning he was up and about unusually early, and was seen bringing water into the house. This he evidently used to thoroughly clean himself in a bid to remove any tell-tale evidence. Later that Saturday evening, after being quizzed by the RUC in Newry, he was examined by a police doctor, who took forensic samples. The medic noted how exceptionally clean McGladdery was and that his skin was a reddish colour as if it had been scrubbed almost raw.

No amount of scrubbing, however, could remove the scratch marks from his skin, which no one could recall having seen the previous evening. Asked how they were inflicted, McGladdery told police a chest expander had slipped, striking him in the face. He wasn't believed, of course, and his home was searched. This yielded a book, Micky Spillane's, *The Long Wait,* which bore star-shaped marks similar to the wounds inflicted on Pearl. These had been caused, it was believed, by the tang (the bit which fits into a wooden handle) of a file. McGladdery, it was known, had bought two files on the Friday for use in a small shoe repairing business he operated from home.

Vital pieces of the evidence jigsaw were still missing, however, including McGladdery's bloodstained clothes and the murder weapon. Convinced they knew their man, the police began to effectively harass McGladdery, constantly watching him and subjecting him to regular questioning. Sooner or later, they believed, he would make a mistake. On 9 February 1961, Constable Donald Keown spotted McGladdery leaving Fallone's cafe in Hill Street and making his way to the Savoy Cinema. The officer waited for him to re-emerge, which he did about 11.20 pm, returning to the cafe. Shortly before midnight, McGladdery, wearing his trademark 'Paddy hat', was again on the move, pausing briefly to talk to someone in Hill Street. Suddenly, without warning, he sprinted away, losing the pursuing constable along the Downshire Road. Constable Keown made his way to McGladdery's house, but he wasn't there. At 12.45 am he arrived home via Damolly Lane.

At daybreak the police moved in to search the area, convinced that McGladdery had been either disposing of evidence or checking that his earlier cover-up was secure. In a field, a little more than 300 yards from McGladdery's house, they discovered an old septic tank. Using a stick to probe the bottom, officers hooked a bag, weighted down by a large stone, from the stinking waters. Inside was an overcoat, vest and handkerchief, all bearing what appeared to be bloodstains. There was also a necktie, believed to have been the murder weapon. McGladdery was promptly arrested.

Pearl's murder had caused outrage across Northern Ireland and, naturally, nowhere more so than in Newry. When McGladdery appeared at the town's courthouse in April it was besieged by a 500-strong crowd, the vast majority of whom were excluded from the courtroom for sheer want of space. Inside there was high drama, with McGladdery's mother, Agnes, attempting to clasp her son's hand as he sat in the dock, only to be restrained by two warders and a policeman. A bid was made to have the trial heard in County Fermanagh because of alleged prejudice and the publication of newspaper articles considered to be in contempt of court. In the event, the trial was held at Downpatrick in October before Lord Justice Curran. His selection was considered controversial by some, as his own daughter, Patricia, had been murdered several years earlier in remarkably similar circumstances. In his opening address, Brian Maginness, the Attorney-General, told the court:

> "The sum total of this evidence points in one direction only – that McGladdery on that early morning of January 28, foully and deliberately murdered this young girl. The taking off of her clothes suggests a sexual motive, and although it is not necessary for the Crown to prove motive, you may come to the conclusion that passion started this affair. And an unrequited passion may have been succeeded by hate or anger."

After five days of evidence, during which the prosecution called fifty-eight witnesses and McGalddery's side just three, the all-male jury took just forty minutes to bring in its verdict of guilty. What hadn't been revealed to them, or the public at that point, was that McGladdery, from an otherwise respectable family, had ten previous convictions, including assault, wounding with intent and possession of a rifle and had served terms of imprisonment in England and Northern Ireland. The execution date was set for 7 November, but was delayed while McGladdery unsuccessfully appealed. Part of his argument had

How the *Northern Whig* reported the end of the court case.

been that some of the reporting about his case, during which he was described as a "self-confessed gunman, safe cracker thief, and general desperado," had made it impossible for him to receive a fair trial. But, if nothing else, he ate well while awaiting his appointment with the executioner. For breakfast the menu offered 12 ozs of bread, half-an-ounce of butter, a pint of porridge, pint of tea, half a pint of milk, an egg with bacon or sausage; dinner was 1 lb potatoes, 8 ozs of bread, 6 ozs of chops, steak, fish or liver, 4 ozs vegetables, one pint of soup and half a pint of rice, sago, cornflour or custard; tea consisted of 12 ozs of bread, half-an-ounce of butter, one pint of tea, half a pint of milk, cheese, jam, cottage pie, rissoles or fish; with half-a-pint of tea and toast for supper. Later corned beef was added to the menu at his request.

The final execution date was set for Wednesday, 20 December 1961, just five days before Christmas, After confessing his guilt to the Presbyterian chaplain, McGladdery, who was given a drop of 5 ft 4 ins, became the last man to be hanged in Northern Ireland. Approximately thirty people gathered outside the gaol on the day of execution. One assumes many more would have made the effort if they had known its significance. At 8.05 am, when a notice declaring that the sentence of death had been carried out was posted on the wicket gate, they moved forward to read it before dispersing. Inside the

A small crowd braved the cold December morning to stand on the Crumlin Road until the notice confirming McGladdery's execution was posted on the jail door. *(News Letter)*

gaol, an inquest held shortly after the execution returned a verdict of death due to the fracture of the cervical spine after judicial hanging. As the soil was returned to McGladdery's unmarked grave within the prison walls, it brought to an end a controversial chapter in the prison's history that is unlikely ever to be reopened.

CHAPTER FOURTEEN

In conclusion

It did stick with me. It was traumatic at the time. It must have been, I suppose, three or four months before I got over it.

A former death watch warder

C ONCERNS OVER CAPITAL PUNISHMENT in the last 150 years of its existence resulted in investigations by two Royal Commissions and two Select Committees. The first sat in 1819, the last from 1949 to 1953. While some raised the odd doubt, they generally endorsed hanging as the best method of dealing with murderers. Arguments on the issue raged elsewhere, of course, and nowhere more fiercely than in Northern Ireland in the wake of the two executions of 1961. Stormont came under tremendous pressure to change the law, with a series of Parliamentary debates showing that the ruling Unionist Party was split on the issue, while the Opposition was almost exclusively anti-noose. Privately, the Cabinet agreed that some reform of the law was necessary, but was reluctant to go public for fear of inflaming both the pro- and anti-hanging lobbies any further.

In November 1963, however, the issue came to a head when Stormont's only Liberal MP, Sheelagh Murnaghan, brought forward a Private Member's Bill, the Homicide and Criminal Responsibility Bill, which included the abolition of capital punishment. Guaranteed the support of Opposition members, the Cabinet feared enough Unionists would also give their backing for it to be passed, and so let it be known it was prepared to bring forward its own proposals. The Murnaghan Bill was subsequently defeated, but only by

Northern Ireland Prime Minister Captain Terence O'Neill, left, with Irish premier Jack Lynch and Brian Faulkner, was under pressure to abolish hanging. *(News Letter)*

four votes. The following year the Northern Ireland Government reaffirmed its commitment to bring forward legislation for the abolition of hanging. At the same time, capital punishment was suspended in Great Britain for an experimental five-year period. The tide had finally turned in favour of those opposed to State executions.

When the Criminal Justice Act, published in 1965 but not passed until the following year, finally came before Stormont, however, it was not as comprehensive as many had wanted. Citing four types of murder still punishable by death, it led to a Unionist revolt that ensured some concessions. In its final form the Bill abolished hanging for "normal" murder, but still applied the ultimate penalty to two categories: the killing of a police officer or Crown servant, or any person assisting them in the execution of their duty, such as prison warders; and killings "in the course or furtherance of any seditious act or conspiracy to further the activities or aims of seditious organisations," or, in other words, terrorist-related murders. If such a law had existed since the creation of the Northern Ireland state, only one man, IRA killer Tom Williams, would have been executed.

Despite its shortcomings, the 1966 Act actually put Northern Ireland ahead of Great Britain, which wasn't to abolish hanging permanently until 1969. It, too, retained exclusion clauses allowing for the execution of those found guilty of treason, arson in Her Majesty's dockyard and piracy on the high seas, with a gallows being retained at Wandsworth Prison. At the Crumlin Road Gaol the scaffold was also intact, and was to remain so for a number of years yet. Although Westminster was unhappy at the anomaly between Great Britain and Northern Ireland, and said so privately, it had to wait another four years before it could do something about it.

With the violence of the late Sixties and early Seventies, it was only a matter of time before a sentence of death was to be again passed in Northern Ireland. That day arrived in February 1973, when Albert Edward Browne, a member of the then legal Ulster Defence Association, was convicted of murdering a policeman in October of the previous year and condemned to be hanged. Mr

Twenty-five years of terrorist violence left its mark on Crumlin Road Gaol. *(News Letter)*

Justice McGonigal, who passed sentence on 29-year-old Browne at the Belfast City Commission, did not don the traditional black cap. The execution date was set for 25 April but, on the 6 April, Secretary of State William Whitelaw used his powers under Section One of the Northern Ireland (Temporary Provisions) Act to commute the sentence to life imprisonment. Browne was told of the decision in the condemned cell at Crumlin Road Gaol. Later that month, a 19-year-old Roman Catholic, William Gerard Holden, was sentenced to death for the murder of a soldier. He also took up residence in the condemned cell, but had not long to wait. A clause inserted in the Northern Ireland Emergency Provisions Bill, bringing the Province's capital punishment laws into line with those applying in Great Britain, came before MPs at Westminster on 15 May, and was overwhelmingly passed. A few hours later, Holden, the last man to be condemned to die by an Ulster court, was told his sentence had been commuted to imprisonment for life. He served

Lord Willie Whitelaw, as Secretary of State for Northern Ireland, incorporated into the Emergency Provision Bill the legislation bringing the Province's laws on capital punishment into line with those operating in Great Britain. *(News Letter)*

Liam Gerard Holden, the last man sentenced to be hanged in Northern Ireland. *(Irish News)*

seventeen years behind bars before he was released on licence in 1989. In 2012 the Royal Court of Appeal overturned his conviction.

The scaffold at the end of C wing in Belfast Prison could, at long last, be dismantled with the room, and the condemned cell next door, being converted to other uses. The gaol burying ground, alongside the garden wall, had received its last body. The political debate over capital punishment, and its possible restoration, had not gone away, however. Barely two years after abolition in Great Britain, a bid was made to bring back hanging. Since then there have been many similar votes in the Commons, but as the years have passed, the Parliamentary majority opposed to restoration has grown.

By 1995 Crumlin Road Gaol itself was under sentence of death. As it marked the 150th anniversary of its completion, the cost of modernising its facilities made retention more expensive than building a replacement while the continuing paramilitary ceasefires lessened the need for such a high level of prison accommodation. A reprieve for the prison appeared unlikely with only an execution date remaining to be set.

In November 1991, two loyalist prisoners named Robert Skey and Colin Caldwell had died as the result of an IRA bomb planted behind a radiator in the C wing dining hall. It was the worst incident of several years of violence between the rival factions over a demand for segregation. A report by Viscount Colville in April 1992, ordered after the bombing, found the regime under which remand prisoners were being held "produces a desolate life" with the constant risk of attack on the stairways, reception area and landings. It added, "The regime is tough – it can not be reasonable that men should have to be put on a list to defecate other than in their cell chamber pot". The report highlighted how prisoners were kept in their cells for up to twenty-three hours, and ate all their meals there; did not have daily access to washing facilities; and were denied education, recreation and gym opportunities.

The disruption in the gaol continued, with rooftop protests, further incidents of violence and even a loyalist rocket attack that damaged the roof of A wing. A rampage by prisoners at the gaol in 1994 resulted in the destruction of many of the cells in A and B wings and led to a mass transfer of inmates to the H-blocks at the Maze, where loyalists and republicans were kept apart. In February 1995 a plan to close Crumlin Road Gaol within three years and transfer prisoners to an extended Maghaberry Prison, near Lisburn, was published. At that time there were just 180 remand prisoners in the gaol and a further 97 sentenced prisoners serving short terms, watched over by some 440 staff. On 31 March 1996, the doors of Crumlin Road Gaol were officially closed for the last time as a place of incarceration with the remaining inmates moved to Maghaberry Prison and Magilligan Prison in County Londonderry. The gaol was kept in "warm storage" for a number of years, its facilities maintained and its kitchen area wrapped in plastic sheeting so that it could quickly be opened up again should the need arise. Part of the gaol was also used to accommodate asylum seekers for a period up to 2004 despite claims that it was a breach of their human rights.

There was no shortage of interest from outside bodies in the Grade A listed building and fourteen acre site following its closure. The Phoenix Trust, which acquired buildings of historical interest and restored them, was said to be looking at the building; development company Dunloe Ewart, which purchased the courthouse for a £1 in 1999, reportedly considered the possibility of turning the prison into a cultural centre; St Malachy's College wanted some of the land for sports facilities; the Mater Hospital proposed spreading on to the gaol site; the charity Bryson House saw the gaol as a possible new headquarters; the Public Record Office of Northern Ireland carried out tests in the cells to gauge its suitability as a storage area with the courthouse on the opposite side of the road being viewed as a potential reading room; the De Bono Foundation, working in conjunction with the Museum of Citizenship, expressed an interest; and Belfast City Council proposed opening a multi-media visitors' centre telling the story of the city's citizens over the past one hundred years.

In May 2002, then Prime Minister Tony Blair unveiled a £200 million funding package for Northern Ireland which included the transfer to the Assembly's Executive of the Crumlin Road Gaol, the Maze prison, Ebrington barracks and army bases at Magherafelt and Malone Road, Belfast. The gaol was opened to the public in September 2005 for two days as part of the European Heritage Open Days and its potential as a visitor attraction was immediately apparent with the 162 places snapped up and more than 500 further enquiries received, including one from Australia. A project to restore the front of the gaol was undertaken in 2007, removing the "modern" security measures, blast walls, razor wire, fencing and bulletproof glass, and repairing and restoring its railings and main gates. That year guided tours, initially twice a week, were introduced and today the prison is one of the most popular attractions for tourists and locals alike. It now houses state-of-the-art conferencing and hospitality facilities, a café and shop. Where once the sounds of crashing doors and barked orders filled the air, you are now more likely to hear clanking champagne glasses and director's instructions as the gaol is available for corporate events, lecturers, wedding receptions, concerts, as a film and television scene location, and temporary cinema or theatre. A whiskey distillery is also planned for the site, the first in Belfast for close on a century. The courthouse, so integrally linked with the gaol, has not faired so well and has suffered from break-ins, considerable vandalism and a number of fires, including one in 2009 that caused major damage.

The final word goes to a man who had more experience of capital punishment than anyone, executioner Albert Pierrepoint. He wrote in his 1974 autobiography:

> "The fruit of my experience has this bitter aftertaste; that I do not now believe that any one of the hundreds of executions I carried out has in any way acted as a deterrent against future murder. Capital punishment in my view, achieved nothing except revenge."

CHAPTER FIFTEEN

Crumlin Road Gaol today

After years obscured behind modern security measures the facade of Sir Charles Lanyon's County Gaol for Antrim is once again revealed.

The view through the entrance of the gate lodge which now contains the gift shop.

The administration building or Governor's House, now also denuded of modern security, is an imposing presence over the courtyard.

The spacious Governor's office within the administration building with the confident presence of the first Governor, John Forbes.

Governors of the prison over the years.

A view of B wing radiating from the central hall, in the style of the pioneering Pentonville Jail.

The view along C wing which eventually housed the permanent execution chamber, complete with watchful guard.

Opposite: Views of both A wing, which originally held the women, and C wing. The three levels of the gaol's design can be clearly seen.

D wing, which runs towards the Mater Hospital, still remains largely unchanged from its state just pre-closure.

The view down one of the stair wells from the top level.

The view along C wing towards the circle where the door into the administration building can just be seen.

One of the original wooden cell doors on display. This type proved too prone to vandalism.

A guard in the Parcels room contemplates the new deliveries destined for inmates.

The Movement Officer's room facilitated this crucial role to ensure every prisoner was accounted for at all times, whether leaving the wing for a visit, hospital or court hearing.

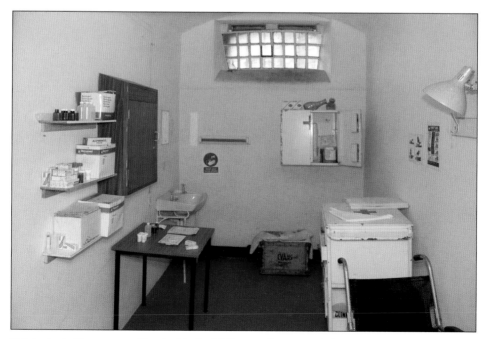

This locked office was used by the Medical Officer to dispense medication to prisoners on the wing.

A re-creation of the original 1846 gaol cell – 7 ft wide and 9 ft 10 in high – and described as having a commode, basin, wooden bed, table, stool, shelves with books, comb, brushes, towels, bedding, soap and gas light. Each cell was for a single person, with the female prisoner here depicted pulling apart old rope.

The 1950s cell still contained a single occupant and furnishings remained similar. The chamber pot had to be emptied every morning, a routine known as 'slopping out'. Prisoners were served their food in the cells.

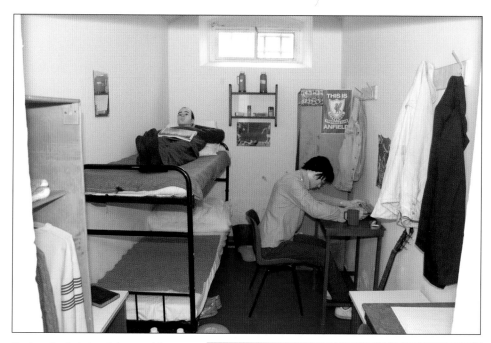

During the height of the Troubles in the 1970s and 1980s, as the prison population grew, up to four men could share a cell. Prisoners were now taken to a dining hall for meals but there was still no sanitation in the cells.

The narrow room, known to the Prison Officers as the 'bacon slicers' and the prisoners as the 'grills', where the prisoners returned from C wing exercise yard. Movement was strictly regulated so that the numbers re-entering the wings could be controlled. Only a couple of prisoners were escorted through to their cells at once so that the guards could not be overwhelmed.

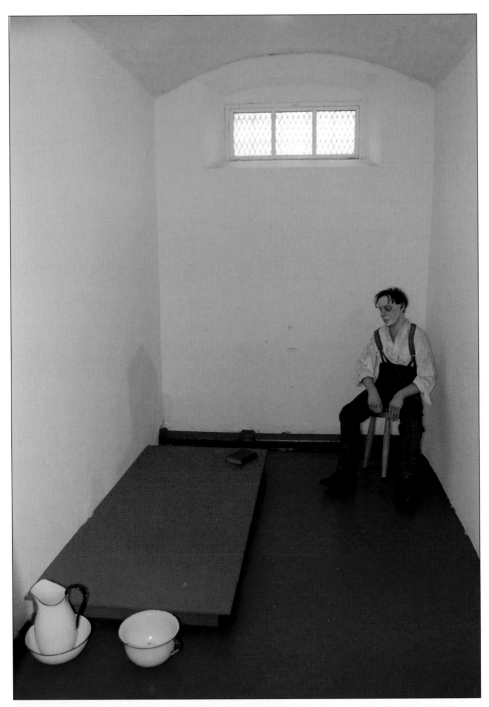

A re-creation of the punishment cell, known as 'the Boards'. There was no furniture and during the day the bedding was removed from the plain board on the floor. The prisoner only had a Bible, water container, mug and chamber pot.

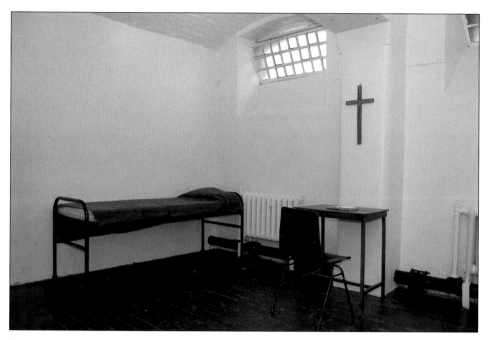

The sparsely furnished condemned cell which was twice as big as a normal cell.

Although basic, it was equipped with washing and toilet facilities.

Included in the toilet facility was a cupboard that hid a door connecting the condemned cell directly to the execution chamber.

The door was revealed only seconds before the execution was to take place. It must have come as a shock to many a prisoner to realise that he had been living and sleeping barely a dozen steps away from the place he was to meet his end.

The permanent execution chamber saved the condemned man from the previous arrangement which involved a harrowing walk along D wing and up several flights of stairs to the gallows.

The permanent gallows at Crumlin Road was in a stone chamber at the very end of C wing. Two trap doors existed – one for the execution and one covering a flight of stairs leading to the inspection room beneath.

The actual process of hanging was governed by a strict set of memorandum from the Home Office. However, the approved hangmen rarely needed to refer to the printed instructions.

The whole operation from the prisoner entering the cell until the freeing of the trap doors took less than half a minute.

The trap doors now always stand open into the room below where the body would hang undisturbed for an hour before being placed in a coffin ready to be inspected by the inquest jury.

The hanged man was placed in a plain rough wood coffin which would be filled with quick lime before being lowered into the ground.

A view of the stone steps leading from the inspection rooms that would take the prisoner to his final burial place within the gaol and behind the garden wall.

A view of the end of C wing showing were the additional chamber was added.

A vew of the exterior of B wing and the water tower that stood above the circulation area.

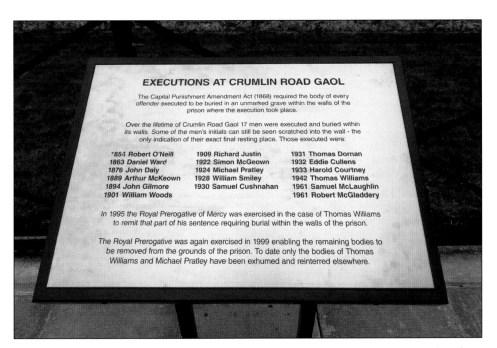

A plaque details the seventeen men who were executed and buried at the Crumlin Road Gaol. Only fifteen bodies still remain.

The stretch of 'garden wall' that marks the spot were the condemned men were buried from 1854 to 1961. Although intended to be unmarked graves, prisoners and sometimes even warders did in fact mark some of the graves by etching names or initials and year of execution onto the wall above the spot.

Michael Pratley, 1924.

Samuel Cushnan, 1930.

Harold Courtney, 1933.

Thomas Williams, 1942.

Samuel McLaughlin, 1961.

The end gable of D wing which faces the Mater Hospital and where the initial hangings at the gaol took place.

The brick tunnel which connected the Crumlin Road Gaol to the Courthouse across the road.

Now in disuse, the central section of the tunnel was strengthened with concrete during the Troubles to protect it from collapse during bomb attacks on the buildings above.

Select Bibliography

Abbot, Geoffrey, *Lords of the Scaffold: A History of the Executioner*, Headline Book Publishing, 1991

Bailey, Brian, *Hangmen of England: A History of Execution from Jack Ketch to Albert Pierrepoint*, Barnes & Noble Books, 1994

Bardon, Jonathan, *Belfast: An Illustrated History*, Blackstaff Press, 1982

Beckett, JC, *The Making of Modern Ireland*, Faber and Faber, 1974

Beckett, JC, et al, *Belfast: the Making of the City*, Appletree Press, 1982

Bell, J Bowyer, *The Secret Army: A History of the IRA 1916-70*, Poolbeg Press Ltd, 1989

Berry, James, *My Experiences As An Executioner*, David & Charles Publishers, 1972

Bleackley, Horace, *The Hangmen of England*, Chapman & Hall Ltd, 1929

Brett, CEB, *Buildings of Belfast, 1700-1914*, Weidenfeld & Nicholson, 1967

Brewer, John, *The Royal Irish Constabulary: An Oral History*, Institute of Irish Studies, 1990

Coogan, Tim Pat, *The IRA*, Roberts Pub Co Ltd, 1993

Dickson, Charles, *Revolt in the North: Antrim and Down in 1798*, Clonmore and Reynolds, 1960

Duff, Charles, *A New Handbook on Hanging*, Andrew Melrose, London, 1954

Gravestone Inscriptions, various volumes, The Ulster-Scot Historical Foundation, Belfast.

Hayes-McCoy, GA, *Irish Battles: A Military History of Ireland*, Appletree Press, 1990

Kee, Robert, *The Green Flag*, Penguin Books, 1991

Koestler, Arthur, *Reflections on Hanging*, AMS Press, 1997

Koestler, Arthur, *Hanged By The Neck*, Penguin, 1961

Larmour, Paul, *Belfast: An Illustrated Architectural Guide*, Friar's Bush Press, Belfast, 1987

Lewis, CS, *The Humanitarian Theory of Punishment*, Marcham Manor Press, 1930

MacColl, Rene, *Roger Casement*, Four Square/Landsborough, London, 1960

Madden, Dr Richard Robert, *Antrim and Down in '98*, Burns Oates & Washbourne, London, 1899

McAllister, James, *A Belfast Chronicle, 1789: A compilation from the News Letter*, Friar's Bush Press, Belfast, 1989

McNeill, Mary, *The Life and Times of Mary Ann McCracken: A Belfast Panorama*, Blackstaff Press, 1988

McNeill, TE, *Anglo-Norman Ulster: The History and Archaeology of an Irish Barony, 1177-1400*, John Donald Publishers, 1980

O'Broin, Leon, *The Unfortunate Mr Robert Emmet*, Clonmore & Reynolds, Dublin, 1958

O'Hanlon, the Rev WM, *Walks Among the Poor of Belfast and Suggestions For Their Improvement*, SR Publishers, 1971

Patton, Marcus, *Central Belfast: A Historical Gazetteer*, Ulster Architectural Heritage Society, 1993

Pierrepoint, Albert, *Executioner: Pierrepoint*, Harrap, 1974

Potter, John Deane, *The Fatal Gallows Tree*, Elek Books, 1965

Scott, George Ryley, *The History of Capital Punishment*, Merchant Book Company, 1996

Sinclair, RJK, and Scully, FJM, *Arresting Memories*, The Royal Ulster Constabulary, Belfast, 1982

Thackeray, William Makepeace, *The Irish Sketch Book, 1842*, Blackstaff Press, 1985

Walker, Brian, and Dixon, Hugh, *No Mean City: Belfast 1880-1914*, Friar's Bush Press, 1983

Walker, Brian Mercer, *Faces of the Past*, Appletree Press, 1974

Wallace, Martin, *Famous Irish Lives*, Irish Books & Media, 1991

Young, Robert M, *Historical Notices of Old Belfast and its Vicinity*, Marcus

Ward & Co, Belfast, 1896

Young, Robert M, *Ulster in '98: Episodes and Anecdotes*, Marcus Ward & Co, Belfast, 1893

Viscount Colville of Culross QC, *The Operational Policy in Belfast Prison for the Management of Paramilitary Prisoners from Opposing Factions*, Stationery Office Books, Belfast, 1992

Newspapers:

Armagh Guardian

Banner of Ulster

Belfast Commercial Chronicle

Belfast Mercury

Belfast Morning News

Belfast Telegraph

Coleraine Chronicle

Irish News

Newry Reporter

Newry Telegraph

News Letter

Northern Whig

Index